Creating Calm

3 Powerful Models for Navigating the Rough Seas of Midlife

by

Vickii Engel Thomas, MS, LMT

Contents

Dedication

This book is dedicated to all those in midlife
willing to transform their lives, creating calm,
joy, and freedom for the journey yet ahead.

Preface

I never longed to write a book or become an author. In first grade I struggled to learn to read, and through high school and college took the minimum number of English and literature courses required. Numbers and equations seemed far friendlier than words and sentences, so I became a math teacher. That preference somehow did not seem to matter to the inspirational voice that took up residence just above my left shoulder. Frequently, while speaking before a community group, lecturing to graduate students, or coaching a client, the little voice would say, "That would be great in the book!" Occasionally, after a presentation, one of the participants would come up and ask, "Have you ever considered writing a book?" For at least the last 15 years, this book has continued to nudge me from the inside and the outside, and I have resisted. Over these same years, I was raising a child, tending a home and family, running two businesses, and writing and teaching graduate counseling courses. That felt like more than enough to do. Yet, the little voice talking about a book did not go away.

In July of 2016, I turned 60. Successfully making my way through the colorful twists and challenging turns of midlife, I realized that two thirds of my life was now behind me. I spent a little time looking back over the last 30 years. The topic of the book again surfaced. Over the years I had written files full of inspiring thoughts and images, but no book. This incompletion stood there, staring back at me like a lifeless salt statue. And while I would rather have been taking a cooking class or volunteering on an organic farm, I committed myself to the living room sofa and my laptop for as long as it took.

This book is written from my own midlife experiences as a therapist and educator, but mostly from my experience as an average human being. I have traveled along with many of my clients and students as they have courageously shared the struggles and stuck places of their own midlife journeys. As I listened, several themes kept reappearing. The first two models presented in this book – the Mobius shift and the Boat and the Breeze – were created out of images and metaphors that emerged from my own experiences and those of others. The third – the Drama Triangle – comes from the work of psychologist Eric Berne in the 1960's and his book *The Games People Play*. The names of people in the examples have been changed to maintain confidentiality, and in many cases, the details of the story are a composite of a number of clients with similar patterns. All are real. All are true. Much of what these tools offer can be applied to all of life, but they are especially appropriate and powerful during the midlife years.

This book was written with my current clients in mind, as well as those ages 35 and beyond, who having set sail on the seas of midlife, are looking for tools to make the voyage calmer, smoother, and more satisfying. My hope is that you, the reader, will find some aspect of these ideas supportive, clarifying, and inspiring, and that they will help make the midlife years a better passage both for yourself and those whose lives you touch. Perhaps you will even have an "Ah-ha!" moment in the process.

Acknowledgements

I wish to extend my *deepest appreciation* to the following folks who have helped me to make this book a reality:

To therapist and intuitive Andrea Bowman who, for most of the last 15 years, continued to suggest ways that might move me beyond my resistance to writing a book.

To my therapists and teachers Judith and Roger Roark, for their openhearted commitment in assisting many others and me in living a more conscious life.

To the hundreds of students and clients who have applied these models in their own lives and enthusiastically shared about the changes they were able to make.

To Mike Koenig and Ed Rush of Publish and Profit, for creating a kick-ass training that helped me shatter my own glass ceiling by turning my ideas about publishing upside down, providing me with both a structure and a deadline.

To my editor Jillian Childs, for her incredibly constructive feedback, inspiring enthusiasm for language, and delightful sense of humor.

To my niece and graphic designer Anne Thompson, for her positive "no problem" attitude and crisp images.

To Jason Jordan of Barnum Media, for his expertise, kindness, and generosity of spirit in helping me birth this book into the digital world.

To Dr. Jay C. Polmar, for his patient coaching with formatting and the book cover design.

To Linda Hylan, for her warm friendship as well as her quick and thorough feedback on the final proof.

To my son Paul Thomas, for his wisdom, wit, and endless patience in getting me up to speed on a Mac.

To my partner Michael Rosner, who reminded me that even if I did not end up publishing a book, it would be an adventure. He was right!

The Mobius Shift of Midlife

"They always say that time changes things,
but you actually have to change them yourself."

– Andy Warhol

During my nine-year career as a mathematics teacher, I realized that what I loved most about being an educator was helping students discover more about who they were as human beings. With that insight, I started taking a few graduate courses in counseling. A year or so later, I had my first massage. After the session, I was absolutely amazed at how well and wonderful I felt, and decided to pursue training out of personal interest. In massage school, I soon learned that much of our personal history was not just stored in our brain as a memory, but was also exquisitely laced throughout our physical body. When the body tissue was gently and respectfully touched during massage, this history could make itself known. Emotions, memories, even unfinished business sometimes came into the person's awareness during a session. Wanting to safely support clients when this history emerged, I returned to graduate school to complete a masters degree in counseling. Now with a background in education, massage therapy, and counseling, I began integrating my skills so that could I offer clients an experience of support for mind, body, and emotion.

Harry (not his real name), a highly paid corporate executive in his 60's, came to my office for an integrative session on his day off. Experiencing physical pain and depression, he felt hopelessly trapped in a job he disliked, but had to maintain in order to sustain the family's standard of living. Outside of work hours, Harry found his time was consumed by meeting family demands, many self-imposed. We made a list of things that inspired and energized him - cycling, hiking, and traveling, among other activities. When I asked when he might take some time to do any one of these, he was silent. "What are you doing today after this appointment?" I asked. "Taking my daughter's car for an emission test and changing the oil." Since the weather was lovely, I asked if he could first go for a hike in the nearby Catoctin Mountains. "No" was Harry's immediate and clear reply. Even though he had the whole day off, he did not have permission within himself to choose something different for himself. He was always focused on the *other* - something that someone else needed or wanted. While he felt exhausted and discouraged to the point of being depressed, he was imprisoned by his old beliefs that the role of a man was to be a provider for his family. Never had he allowed himself to include himself in the long list of those for whom he was providing. While trying to nudge Harry to do something - anything - for himself, the image of a Mobius strip popped into my head. I grabbed a sheet of paper and a pair of scissors and cut a thin strip to demonstrate.

The Mobius Shift

You too can do this right now. Get a sheet of paper and cut a strip of paper approximately 8 inches long and ½ inch wide. (Seriously, do it right now. It will make this much easier to understand.) On one side of the slip, write the word "others" three or four times. On other side, write "self" three or four times. On the *self* side put a small star at **both** ends. Now put the ends of the strip together so that it makes a paper circle with the word *others* on the outside and *self* on the inside.

This paper circle models the way many of us live the first part of our lives. The *others'* needs come first. They are visible and easy to see. Our own needs, or that of the *self*, are secondary and best kept hidden on the inside. We believe this is how things are supposed to be. This belief, like most of our core beliefs, is formed when we are very young and generally by the time we are seven years of age. There is nothing wrong with putting others first. The difficulty is that buried in this belief is an implied *always* – I must *always* put others' needs first. This belief then offers us only one option – others come first at all times.

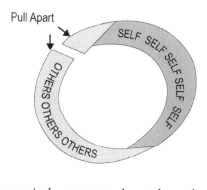

Holding the paper circle, separate the ends so the circle begins coming apart. Turn **one end** completely over or upside down. Move the ends of the circle back together again. (The stars should now literally touch.)

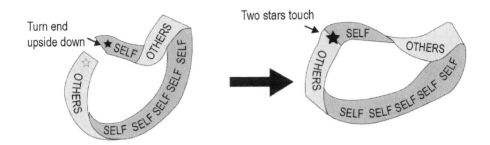

This paper loop is no longer a circle with two sides – inside and outside. It is a called a Mobius strip, commonly known as an "infinity loop." Mathematically speaking, it is a one-sided plane. The paper strip previously had two sides – a front and a back. When you flipped just one end and attached again to the other end, you actually eliminated one side. Now the paper strip has only *one* side.

To experience this, let your finger slide along the curve marked *self*. As you move forward, your finger will slide right onto the side marked *others*. If you continue moving along, your finger will slide again across the part labeled *self*. You can travel from one side to what had been the opposite without lifting your finger or turning the paper over. There really is no longer an inside and outside like in the paper circle. In essence, there is only *one* side. This is the magic of a Mobius strip! I consider this the perfect model of the transformation offered to each of us during our middle years. I call it the "Mobius Shift of Midlife." This shift takes place in at least seven significant ways; let's take a closer look at each of these.

From Selfish to Self-care

In 1988, I had just finished my certification training in massage therapy, and "stress management" was the catch phrase of the day. At the time, many of my clients were women, giving me the chance to hear about the challenges for women in a wide variety of work and life styles. During the first appointment, I would ask about their stress level and how they were managing it. As I watched, I noticed that they would look about as if searching for an answer that was floating just above their head. The question invariably took them out of a felt experience in their body and into to a cognitive wandering through their imaginary appointment book, looking for the last time they had done something that managed their stress. I quickly learned that using the phrase "stress management" took clients in the wrong direction. Rather than recall a physical experience that created relief, they went into thought. Not long after that, I came upon the phrase "self-care," revised my health intake form, and began asking clients how they took care of themselves. This time I noticed that instead of looking dazed and detached, the question stopped them dead in their tracks. "I don't. I can't do that! If I take care of myself, who will take care of the children, the laundry, my aging father"…(Dinner dishes, the boss, the mail, the church meeting minutes. You get the picture.) "Besides, if I took time to take care of myself, I would be *selfish*." There it was – one of the most limiting beliefs on the planet sitting in my office. In midlife, this belief really seems to gain strength and has the potential to create enormous tension and strain at many levels.

Most clients had learned, or somewhere had taken on the belief, that *self-care* meant being *selfish*. Their job was to take care of others, not themselves. Putting themselves first was selfish, and selfish was not something they were ever going to be. It was simply not acceptable. Once while giving a talk at a senior center, I proposed that as a small act of self-care, a woman might serve herself first at dinnertime. A 70-year old woman sitting next to her husband in the second row, audibly gasped and said aloud, "I could never do that! That would be selfish. I always give him dinner first!" She seemed shocked at the very idea. Clearly, it had never been an option for her.

For those who allowed themselves to imagine some act of self-care, guilt, the evil cousin of selfish, would generally move in. Students in my graduate courses have shared that they might long to have a date with a spouse, a quiet hour for painting with watercolor, or just time alone while the kids are still in school. They may even have had the full support of a spouse or their family, but their own inner voice stopped them short. Clients, who paid for my insights and coaching, said the same. A working mother of three made an appointment a month in advance so that she could arrange for her husband to tend the children while she had a massage. After reviewing her health intake and hearing about the strain and exhaustion she was experiencing while trying to keep up with the demands of both her business and the family household, she shared that she also felt guilty coming for the massage. She felt she did not have the time to do a good job at either her business or family life and should be using this time to take care of those responsibilities. She felt guilty taking time to get relief from the physical pain that all the demands created. Students and clients alike agree that self-care is not selfish, but they still feel resistant and sometimes are unable to take action on their own behalf. After embracing the idea, guilt often becomes the next barrier.

One therapist with whom I worked defined guilt as "joy that has been trapped by fear." The desire for something one wants or the joy of tending one's own needs is, in essence, trapped by the fear that by doing so one is selfish, and therefore it is wrong and not allowed. Joy bound by fear creates the stalemate experience of guilt – a virtual internal prison and an exhausting place to live. Our choices are based on our beliefs, both conscious and unconscious, which not only live in our thoughts, but are also laced through our body. In our early years, the possibility of either being viewed as selfish or feeling guilty frequently sinks all hope of choosing self-care.

In midlife, our beliefs about being selfish and guilty are invited to turn upside down, just like the end of the paper circle. When we allow ourselves to turn the belief that self-care is selfish upside down, we give ourselves access to the possibility of having our needs met in many wonderful ways. As we shift this belief, we open up to things not allowed before, from options previously off limits.

From Others to Self

We all need a starter set of beliefs with which to engage the world around us. When we are born, our family of origin, community, religious group, and culture offer us guidelines or rules of what are acceptable thoughts, emotional expressions, and behaviors. These guidelines and rules repeat within us, becoming our own beliefs about who we think we are and how we are to interact with others in our world. In our childhood, these beliefs generally work fairly well, allowing us to remain an accepted part of our family and community. Be nice. Work hard. Always be friendly. Do what you are told. Don't be angry. The problem is that this is just a starter set. None of us are ever told that as we mature in later years, we will need to revise and rewrite some of these beliefs if we want satisfying lives.

An old and hidden belief from my starter set is one that could have been said to me, or manufactured on my own: "When serving dessert, give guests and others the best piece." In my 40's one Sunday afternoon while serving cake, I noticed I was becoming quite irritated for no apparent reason. I suddenly became conscious that I wanted the piece of cake I had just handed to my husband. In my eyes, that was the best piece, but I had no permission to save it for myself. My husband, who seemed a bit baffled by my agitation, simply wanted a piece of cake. He didn't care which one. To him, any piece was fine. The reality was that I was not really able to save any piece for myself - the best or otherwise. Others had to be served first; I got what was left. Even though this belief about serving a dessert seemed rather small and silly, it actually ran a good deal of my thinking and many of my behaviors. I realized that in many other circumstances, I felt compelled to give away what I deemed the best to someone else, regardless of my own wishes or desires. I felt obliged and trapped by this inner mandate, even if others suggested I do otherwise.

Listening to clients over the years, I have come to understand that most of us hold some beliefs that trap us in repeated behaviors *even when we know* they are not good for us. "Others come first" is a belief that is held by many who seek support through counseling. (Though perhaps less common, it is important to note that some people grow up holding the belief that their needs come first. In midlife, their work then is to learn to put others first. They have a slightly different journey, but it is still one of transformation. It still requires a Mobius shift.)

As midlife approaches and the demands of our life increase, most of us feel the strain of life with some of those early beliefs. Some beliefs work just fine for our entire life; generally though, there are at least a few that need to be overhauled. Each needed change often starts with a little feeling of discontent. Our life begins to feel a bit off, not quite right or satisfying. In time, the feeling often moves into restless discomfort, grows ever more annoying, and can eventually develop into a major source of pain before we recognize our now outdated belief. We try our best to continue operating using the beliefs and behaviors of our earlier years, but try as we might, it frequently does not work. Circumstances have changed. The players are different. Needs are different. We work harder, longer, and more committedly to get the job done. Operating our lives with outdated beliefs is a lot like continuing to wear the clothes we wore when we were five years old. They fit fine then, but now they are too tight and only create pain. As we keep trying to live according to these too tight beliefs, we can become frustrated, exhausted, discouraged, depressed, or dis-eased.

Like the paper circle that gets pulled apart and transformed into a Mobius strip, in midlife our life comes apart and gets turned upside down with major life events. This coming apart and turning upside down gives us each the chance to re-evaluate our beliefs and make change. This Mobius shift in midlife gives you a chance to clean house. Old beliefs that no longer serve you can be replaced with ones that now allow you the option of choosing self or others based on the present circumstances. The guidelines, rules, and required behaviors of the past are no longer the only way. You now have the power of choice. One moment you can put your own needs first. The next moment another's needs come first. Like the reconnected curves of the Mobius strip, all needs flow together in one fluid movement. You have both permission and power to choose what is most important in any given moment. This is a powerful place from which to create whatever may be needed or wanted!

From Familiar to Unfamiliar
(or Accepting the Way Life Turned Out)

As midlife turns our life upside down, we are forced to put it back together in some strange new way. "This is not the way I thought my life was going to be" is what I hear from many midlife clients. We find that the only way to move forward is to go into the unknown and to do things we have never before done. It requires us to ditch some of our old beliefs for new ones. If, in the past, we always hid our anger, we may now find it impossible not to speak out. If we planned to retire by age 55, unexpected financial twists may keep us working for additional years. If we married for life, we might find that the healthier choice is to divorce. If we were able to stay at home with children and out of the work force, we may now need to find a job. Many things change in ways we did not want or expect. Some of our early beliefs, like "others first," become a weight that drowns or a prison that enslaves us. Even so, fear of change often rears its head. We attempt to cling to the old known ways of operating. Few of us were raised to embrace the unfamiliar. Unfamiliar was the stranger, and unsafe. We were taught to stay away from this unsafe stranger. In midlife, often we find that making friends with change, the unfamiliar stranger, is the *only* way forward. So, at times shaking with fear, we do that which we have never done. We allow ourselves to change a belief, perhaps even putting our own needs first.

At first it may feel all wrong. The early belief of *others first* does battle with *self first*. But each time we make this new choice and allow this new belief to gain a little ground, we move a little further along the Mobius strip on the curve of Self. Perhaps for the first time we speak up about an injustice we see in our work place. Maybe we look for a new job that gives us energy and respect. Perhaps we finally say "no" to a request for our time when we have no more to give. Perhaps we at long last say "yes" to the gnawing need for solitude and time away from our family. Perhaps we end a friendship in which we were frequently disrespected. Whatever this new and unfamiliar choice is, this new direction in which we did not want or expect to go, it takes us further around the flowing curves of the midlife Mobius strip. Once we move into the new and unfamiliar, we will find ourselves eventually back in the land of familiar. With the Mobius shift of midlife, the flow between them becomes seamless.

From External to Internal

Bill (not his real name), age 49, was a self-employed accountant. He always worried that he and his wife would not have enough money saved for retirement. Bill loved his work, often coming in early and staying late to accommodate his clients' schedules. During Bill's college career, he had worked in a variety of restaurants, learning from each chef so that now he could easily cook creative and delicious dishes at home. Though his wife did none of the cooking, she loved having guests for fancy meals. Bill did all the work before and after dinner parties. He and his wife were frequently invited to parties and always took a wonderful dish. Friends had come to expect this. Since they had no children to tend, his extroverted wife loved to fill their weekends with activity. Bill, by nature, was more of an introvert, but over their 20 years of marriage, he had allowed his wife's preferences to both dictate and fill his weekend time.

Bill arrived at his appointment with acute back and neck pain. In recent months, he had neglected his exercise routines. A month before he had been helping a neighbor unload mulch and plant new shrubbery when his back went out. Then his symptoms of fibromyalgia flared up. In recent weeks, he felt increasingly irritable and resentful. I had worked with Bill for many years, and this pattern was well known to both of us. For much of his life, he had consistently put others' needs first. He recognized that what he longed for most was to be valued and respected. This belief had kept him working too long at the office, cooking meals he did not want to make, volunteering when he really needed to rest, and giving up his much needed free time to please his wife. His body was starting to speak louder, demanding that he stop giving so much away. He had sought his value in doing for others, but he was not valuing or respecting himself. He had gone over his own threshold, and the cost to his body and emotions now had his attention.

Truly valuing ourselves by carefully deciding how we really want to use our time and talents is yet another aspect of the Mobius shift which midlife brings. In the first third of our life, we often gain our worth, acceptance, or value from parents who love us, from friends who say we are part of their group, from an employer who tells us we are doing a great job, and/or from society when we earn a certain level of income. There are many ways we seek a sense of being acceptable that is outside of ourselves. This external orientation established in relation to others is normal and healthy in early life. In the transition at midlife, this is no longer enough. It is not enough that the external world says we are valuable. Our value must come from within, regardless of the external world's opinion. Midlife calls us to shift to an internal point of reference, looking deeply within for our sense of self and self worth. Rather than depend upon others to tell us we are acceptable, we must accept ourselves. Rather than gain our sense of worth from doing for others, we are asked to feel good about ourselves even when we do nothing for others.

From Always & Never to Sometimes

Another Mobius midlife shift is our use of the absolutes *always* and *never*. When my son was little, I would pick him up at school in the afternoons and head home. He'd go out to play and I would go to the kitchen to prepare dinner, wash dishes, and tend the many invisible things that keep a household running. Usually about 5:30 or 6:00 pm, my lower back would start to hurt, sometimes quite significantly. I remember very distinctly my internal conversations. I really wanted to lie down and rest to relieve the pain. My body needed a break, but my head held a belief that said, "Always get your work done first. Then you can rest." Over time, most of us discover that the work will never be all done. We also realize if the work is never done, it means we never get to rest, and most certainly never get to play.

Night after night, I would stand at the sink washing dishes in pain. No one was telling me that I had to do the dishes at that moment. My husband was at work and wouldn't be home for hours. There was no reason that I couldn't lay down for a few minutes, but I simply would not allow myself. I was run by the belief that the work had to come first. One evening when the pain got great enough, I finally said to myself, "That's it! I am going to rest now!" I stretched out on the sofa, propped up my feet, and gave myself ten minutes just to lie there. My head immediately started running a steady stream of negative commentary. "What are you doing? Is this how you're going to waste your time? You know you have so much more to do!" It took some practice, but every time I decided to take a break and rest when in pain, the choice got a little easier. I was able to choose this bit of self-care with far less resistance and far less inner criticism. Gradually, my old belief of "Always get your work done first" was replaced with a more flexible one that allowed me the option of responding to my body's needs as they arose.

This is an example of the common process most of us go through to change a belief. I have heard it many times from both students and clients: changing a belief is work and generally feels like an internal wrestling match. It is simple but hard. Because of this, we often hold on to beliefs even when we know they should change. Sometimes the old belief works in some present circumstances, which also makes us think it is worth keeping. Sometimes, the work actually does have to come first- but not *always*. Often we have far more leeway than we think. I do it one way today tomorrow I might choose another way. I put myself first this time – next time I might choose the others first. In midlife, we are called to release the absolutes of *always* and *never* whenever and wherever they show up. Letting go of the *always* and *never* mentality means we are free to evaluate what is important at any given moment as it unfolds in the here and now. Moving our attention out of the past and into the present moment helps us care for ourselves in a manner that is appropriate for now. It means we can engage with the life that we are actually living, not with a circumstance of the past.

From Either/Or to Both/And

Sometimes beliefs we hold from our early life are bound up in the language of the either/or rule. *Either* I clean the entire house *or* I don't clean any of it. *Either* I take care of others *or* I take care of myself. *Either* I am a good *or* bad. It is a black and white, all-or-nothing mindset. In midlife, this *either/or* mindset of black and white decision-making must shift to that of *both/and* to allow for a variety of potential shades of gray in between. Rather than fulfilling one request *or* the other, can I find a way to fulfill *both*? Ultimately, can I find that middle choice where *both* my needs *and* those of others are satisfied? This becomes a major midlife practice. All decisions can be run through this new belief creating a calm win/win for all.

Marie (not her real name), age 49, came to a session tense and anxious about the upcoming holiday season. Each Christmas, one member of her family hosted the holiday gathering and this year it was her turn. Marie lived in a moderately sized house, but hosting 29 people for a meal was difficult. The floor plan of her home did not allow for an easy flow for serving dinner between the kitchen and living room, and there was limited room to add additional seating. When she was the host for previous holidays, Marie worked hard for several weeks planning and organizing, rearranging furniture, and preparing food in advance, so that it was easier on the day of the gathering. Still, she found herself absolutely exhausted both physically and emotionally when it was over. No matter how much she attempted to be more efficient in her planning, she felt ill for several days when the Christmas dinner was over. On one hand, Marie felt pressure to keep the family tradition going, but on the other, she grew more and more challenged with the expectation. If other family members could manage the holiday meal, why couldn't she? In the weeks preceding the event, the stress she felt manifested in the physical patterns of a rapid heartbeat, headaches, disturbed sleep, and increased agitation.

As I listened to her story, I could hear the either/or in her belief about the holiday meal. *Either* she hosted the meal at her home like everyone else *or* she felt that she was not doing her part to maintain the family tradition. I shared with her the *either/or* in the description of her story, suggesting we explore a way to shift this situation to a both/and, where *both* she could host the dinner *and* feel well when it was over. Marie said she had never thought about it in that way, but was willing to consider another option. The factor that seemed to cause her the most strain was the size and layout of her home. I suggested that she invite her family to her home for appetizers and drinks, arrange the actual dinner meal to be enjoyed at a nearby restaurant that could seat everyone, and then return to her home for desserts and coffee. She liked the idea and proposed it to her family, who were initially hesitant, but willing to try it. A few weeks later Marie arrived for another appointment, reporting that the *both/and* option had worked out quite well. Everyone seemed to adapt to the new dinner arrangement and she woke the following day happily rested with plenty of energy.

Once we recognize that we are trapped in a circumstance by an *either/or* belief, we can literally think outside of the box it keeps us in. Doing so allows us to create a win-win option so that everyone's needs are met. This shift is essential in midlife.

From Alone to All One

Mathematically speaking, a Mobius strip is a one-sided plane. With the twist of one end of the strip, gone is the split duality of two sides; unity is created. This oneness is among the teachings of all spiritual traditions – that we are all connected, all one. The Mobius strip shows us how you and I and all others become one.

Going into the land of self-care, many people are afraid that they will be all alone if they choose to take better care of themselves. At times I have heard from clients that if they make this change, they will be ostracized or rejected, that they would be breaking unspoken rules. This is not the way things are done in their family or community. In choosing self-care, we are often departing from some of the behaviors of a group from which we have belonged, and we may feel a sense of being out there on our own.

But take a deeper look at the nature of the word "alone." It is built from "all" and "one." Allowing ourselves to move into this place of *alone* allows us to more deeply become *all one* with ourselves. It is in the turning over of the end of the paper strip and the moving forward into the curves of the now one-sided Mobius plane that we move from *alone* to *all one*. This shift creates create a rich and powerful connection of unity in any group to which we belong. We do not hold ourselves apart from the group whom we are tending. We give ourselves the same considerations that we give others. When we do this, we create the possibility of being of service to **all**, ourselves included. We have the option of including ourselves on the list of those for whom we care. We know at some level if we do not replenish or recharge ourselves, we run dry. We also know it is impossible to drink from a dry well. Tending our own needs means that we are nourished and energized and therefore able and available for needs of others. With this Mobius shift in midlife, gone is separation. In this way, we become all one.

Enough Pain, Enough Support

What does it take for us to change? One of the students in my graduate counseling course summed it up quite nicely. "We change when we have two things – enough pain and enough support." Consider pain your teacher, who through the experience of sensation, informs you that something in your life needs to change. Each of us must decide our pain threshold. How much pain do we need before we are willing to make the needed change? How long do we let it go on? Where do we find the support? Most changes do not have deadlines. We can make the change or not. For each of us the invitation to change some aspect of our life is just that – an invitation. It often starts with a bit of a whispered idea, gaining in volume and frequency the longer we linger with the invitation.

Over 30 years of self-employment, I have had to increase my session fees numerous times. For me, this has meant two things: first, I would have to value my time and work enough to ask others to pay more for it; second, I would have to muster the courage to look clients in the eyes and say that next

CREATING CALM   Vickii Engel Thomas, MS, LMT

time they came for an appointment, they would have to pay me more. Both aspects were difficult. The first time I needed to increase my fees, I struggled for months internally, negotiating with the inner voice that said that I was asking too much. As I delayed, a nagging impatience would grow. The longer I delayed, the stronger the inner conflict became. I would find that I was thinking about the fee increase repeatedly throughout the day. Knowing that this needed to be done continued to invade more and more of my thought. Sometimes it would wake me up at night. An inner debate would ensue, one side explaining why the increase was appropriate, the other stating why it was not. This inner wrestling match created a great deal of turmoil and consumed an enormous amount of energy.

While the inner wrestling match carried on, I also sought support by talking with other therapists, checking their current fees and finding out how they informed clients. In each conversation, I could hear in their response the value they placed on themselves and the work they did with their clients. I could feel their confidence and clarity about their own work, and their reassurance that, given my training and experience, the increased fee was certainly appropriate.

Now in "enough pain" and having gathered confidence to establish "enough support," I would set a date for the fee increase and share it with clients. What a relief! The conflict ended. Everything inside calmed down. Most clients were completely fine with it. A few asked for a delay due to their own financial circumstances. Occasionally, a client decided to work with another therapist who charged less. All of their responses were perfectly fine. The difficulty was within me, not in their responses. In the process, what I found to be essential was that I listened to my inner wisdom of what was appropriate for me. As years moved along, I found that I had a choice of either creating resistance to what needed to be done or taking action to make it happen. I tried to reduce the lag time from onset of awareness to actually making the change. The sooner I shifted, the more quickly I created calm within myself.

I have seen many clients make a similar shift over the course of our work together. First they recognize that they are struggling, and want to explore ways to get around the concern without changing. As the difficulty increases, their struggle increases; more exploring of small change occurs. At some point as they walk into my office, I can see it on their face and feel it in their presence– they have had enough pain and they are ready for the last round of support in order to shift the beliefs and behaviors that will set them free.

The relief that such a shift brings is palpable. Every cell in the body recognizes a sense of ease and freedom. Shoulders drop. Headaches disappear. Stomach pain evaporates. Anxiety, depression, and agitation resolve into calm, like a still lake on a gentle summer day.

Creating Calm with the Midlife Mobius Shift

The nature of midlife forces us to look at the way we have lived. Any aspect of our life may become the focal point of change. Our home life may be sent into chaos by a severe illness. A growing business can be faced with economic collapse. A marriage might get turned upside down with divorce. We could be fired from a job with a mortgage and a child's college tuition on the horizon. For some, it is a turbulent internal process as they struggle to overhaul their beliefs and to fall in love again with a life they already have. For some, it is a quieter series of subtle events that take them deeply into the places they did not expect to go. Go we must, in a direction we did not anticipate. Regardless of its nature, in midlife, something will turn our world on its head. It is supposed to. If we understand that this is a natural part of a normal midlife, we have a much better chance of working with rather than fighting what shows up.

In summary, midlife is a grand season of life transformation and brings both numerous and continuous opportunities for change. I have described what I consider seven major midlife shifts that we are invited to make during these middle years.

Seven Midlife Shifts

Selfish	...	Self-care
Others	...	Self
Familiar	...	Unfamiliar
External	...	Internal
Always/Never	...	Sometimes
Either/Or	...	Both/And
Alone	...	All One

While I think it is a normal human behavior to resist as these issues arise, we can minimize our stress and strain if we allow ourselves to remember the model of the Mobius strip. We do not have to make midlife difficult or a crisis, but we *do have to change*. We do have to re-evaluate some of our beliefs, rewriting them so that they now fit life as it really is.

Years ago I came upon a book by Brian Luke Seaward titled *Stressed is Desserts Spelled Backwards*. I loved that these two words were a mirror of each other. That's what we need to do in midlife. Like the Mobius strip, we need to turn some things in our life around backwards, doing the thing in a way we have never done it before. Can we put some of life's desserts first? Can we put ourselves first? Can we let go of the absolutes of *always* and *never*, as well as the black and white barriers of *either/or*? Are we willing to drop the illusion of *alone* so that we can become *all one* with the world?

When we remember that the nature of midlife is change, that our life *will* turn upside down, that we can still move forward by allowing our beliefs to shift; these shifts create possibilities we have never dreamed of before. Ultimately, when we allow our lives to flow with these shifts, the rough seas of midlife can resolve into the calm waters of peace, freedom, and even joy.

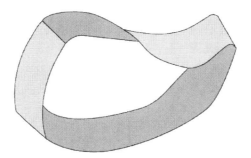

Using the Mobius Shift Model in Your Own Life

Below is a list of questions to help you explore these midlife shifts in your own life. I highly recommend that you *feel* your answer to each one before you *think* about it. Pick one or two questions and journal your answer. Discuss them with a friend. If you are currently working with a counselor or psychotherapist, these are wonderful questions to bring to the sessions. They will help deepen your exploration into your own belief system. As you discover the beliefs that run your life, you create the opportunity to rework them so they are appropriate for the life you are living in your middle years. When the beliefs that govern your life meet the needs in your present life circumstances, you create calm within yourself.

1. What did you imagine midlife would be like for you? What is actually happening in your midlife journey?

2. Like the Mobius shift, in what ways has midlife turned your world upside down?

3. Do you put your needs first? How often?

4. Do you own any always/never beliefs? Are you willing to rewrite them using "sometimes"?

5. Do you own any either/or beliefs? Are you willing to shift to a both/and option?

6. What do you do to take care of yourself? List your ten favorite things.

7. How often do you *do* any of these?

8. How often do you *want to do* any of these?

9. What gets in your way of doing it? What other priorities arise within you?

10. What is the *best time of the day* for this self-care?

11. What is the *best day of the week* for this self-care?

12. Are you willing to literally add this self-care to your schedule?

13. Do you want to hold yourself accountable for doing it? How will you do so?

MODEL #2

The Boat and the Breeze

"When we are no longer able to change a situation,
we are challenged to change ourselves."

Viktor Frankl

Life is quite a ride. Midlife especially has many unexpected ups and downs, twists and turns, pleasures and challenges. Today's popular press talks a great deal about the need for a balanced life and offers many things you can do to take better care of your mind, your body, your emotions, and sometimes your spirit. Nearly every magazine talks about these dimensions and how to create a sense of balanced wellness.

Over my years as a therapist, the question of creating a better balance in life has been a primary one for my clients. This second tool, a sailboat model, evolved from images, ideas, and inspirations gathered over many years, gradually pieced itself together. Focusing on the boat and breeze has helped many clients understand what to do when they feel like they are swimming in emotion or drowning in thought. Visually, it offers a perspective of the dynamics at play in the experience of being human.

To be human and alive means we are in a constant state of flux and movement at many levels. Movement is what the body, with all its joints, ligaments, and muscles, is literally designed for. Movement is what our emotions and thoughts are best at. Movement requires change and change rocks our boat. At some point we each realize that the waves of change in life do not stop. No matter how much we wish for things to stay the same, they simply do not. Change is the eternal constant. Learning to calmly navigate change is essential if we want to live well on the high seas of our very human life. Let's explore this dynamic model beginning with the sailboat itself.

The Boat

You come into this world and you get a body. One. That's it. It has to last a lifetime. Consider your body your one and only sailboat. Looking more closely at how your boat was built, the blueprint for your boat came from your parent's gene pool. When your boat body was crafted in your mother's womb over nine months, her diet, emotions, experiences, and lifestyle dictated the quality of the building materials. Once born, the food you were fed, the touch you received, and the experiences with others in your environment continued to influence the design and functioning of your sailboat. By the time you arrive in adulthood, your body boat's structure and design have been well established.

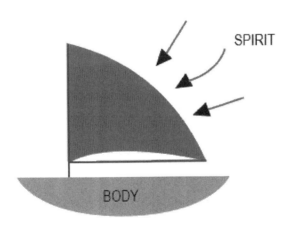

The Breeze

In this model, I consider the wind or breeze the aspect of *spirit* within our lives. Spirit, as it is used here, is all that inspires us and gives our lives meaning and purpose. Spirit includes our connection to others, our sense of community and belonging, whether that is to family, friends, organizations, or clubs. If we have religious traditions or practices, these too are part of this spiritual dimension of being human. I also consider the dimension of spirit to include the sudden insights, intuitions, and synchronicities that add richness and spontaneous sparkle to the flow of our interactions and life.

The Captain and Crew

At the helm of your boat is the captain, your awareness, making decisions based upon all information that comes from the crew as well as the wind and the water. Captain Awareness, as I like to call him or her, is not just in your head. Different from your brain and thoughts, this captain is a bigger presence, a larger consciousness of your self that is more generally aware of information coming from all dimensions of your life. In the current language and teaching about the practice of meditation, this awareness is sometimes referred to as the "observer". Captain Awareness's job is to observe and synthesize all of this information, making wise decisions in order to navigate the high seas of life. His or her job is not only to keep you afloat, but also get you where you want to go safely, smoothly, and calmly.

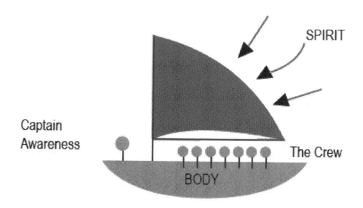

Your boat has seven crewmembers that are tuned in to the finer workings of specific areas of your boat body. These seven crewmembers are in different areas, or wisdom centers, of your body, gathering information and reporting back to the captain through image, sensation, and the function of each center. For example, the crewmember in your heart's wisdom center may report a sensation of warmth when you are with someone you love. When you are anxious, the crewmember in your stomach center may signal that the function of your digestion is disturbed. Each crewmember monitors a different aspect of your body boat, sending information to the captain to incorporate while navigating your boat. If you are familiar with the chakra system, you will recognize the wisdom centers as the seven primary chakras along the spine. If you are not familiar with the chakras, do not worry. Just think of them as various areas of your body, each one with its own information to share. If you want to know more about each chakra, there is no shortage of information available in book form or via Internet sources.

Location of your crewmembers:
>Crewmember #1 – Pelvis/legs/feet
>
>Crewmember #2 – Lower belly
>
>Crewmember #3 – Upper belly
>
>Crewmember #4 – Chest/heart/lungs
>
>Crewmember #5 – Throat
>
>Crewmember #6 – Head and brain
>
>Crewmember #7 – Crown of your head

Captain Awareness relies on all the information from each of the crewmembers, as well as what is happening with the water, waves, and wind. Based on all these combined factors, the captain decides what is needed to sail ahead. The main idea is that your awareness is constantly receiving information from various aspects of your being, especially your physical body. If your captain and crewmembers establish clear and regular communication, he/she can make skillful decisions in navigating the waters of life in a safe, calm, and healthy way.

Setting Sail

Sailboats are lovely, but on dry land, their potential is not realized. On dry land, sailboats become no more than expensive lawn ornaments or monuments to possibilities. They offer little in the way of exploration or adventure. Sailboats are designed to interact with water – to float, to move, to glide - as the sails engage the wind. So think about your body and your life in this way – your body is your sailboat designed to sail with the spirit breeze on the oceans and seas of your life, exploring the nature of being human.

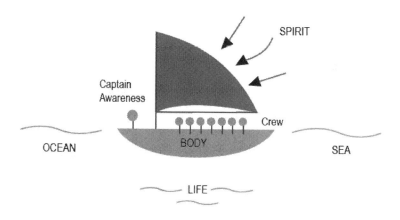

As a child, you and your young Captain Awareness learn to sail your boat around small lakes where the shoreline is in clear view. Rescue teams, like family and friends, are often within sight if the waters get rough and you find yourself in distress. As you grow into adult life, you haul your boat to a larger expanse of water - let's say a bay. With its tributaries, hidden coves, and wide channels, you find much more to explore and more sailing skills to practice. Still, land is often in sight and a safe harbor within reach. By the time you move into midlife, your sailboat has headed into the open waters of the ocean, out of view of dry land. Out here, the wind is much stronger and the waves much higher. Rarely is a rescue team or dry land nearby. Your captain's sailing skills determine whether you arrive at your desired destination, get tossed about aimlessly, or actually sink. In this model, the waves are your emotions and thoughts in your life. Like a sailboat on the open seas, emotions and thoughts rock your boat. The dynamic forces of emotions and thoughts, of water and wave, are the aspects that make navigating the high seas of your life both interesting and challenging. Understanding the dynamic nature of water and wave is essential.

The Ocean of Emotion and the Sea of Thought

In the image below, allow the water to the left of the sailboat to represent your emotions– an ocean of them. The water on the right side of the boat represents your thoughts– a sea of these. Sometimes the waves on the ocean of emotion and sea of thought are calm, reflective, and tranquil. With a sure and steady wind, sailing on these glassy bodies of water is relaxing and easy. Your day goes well, flowing smoothly as you work and play and interact with people in your life.

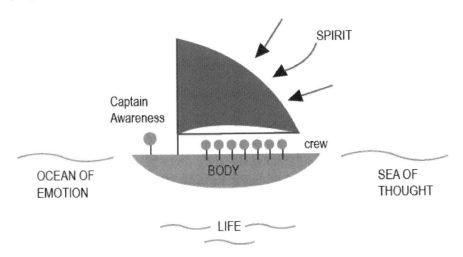

But we know that oceans and seas are not always like that. Most of the time there is much more happening that influences the surface of the water. Winds blow harder, making it choppy and rough, and the sailing requires more effort and skill to stay afloat. Undertows, riptides, and sunken debris hidden beneath the surface can also pull you off course. When the waves are wild and dramatic, expert sailing skills are needed to keep the boat from sinking. On the most challenging of oceans, rogue waves or tsunamis can emerge with a shift in the ocean floor.

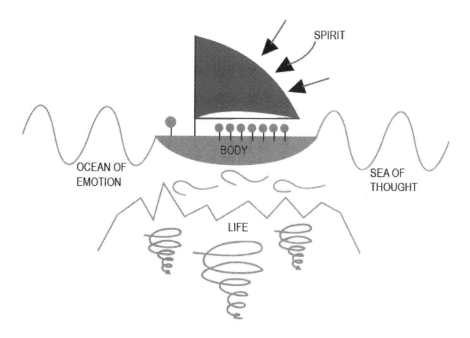

Without Captain Awareness or the skills of your crew, you will go somewhere, but it is not likely to be the direction that you were hoping for. You must both pay attention to and understand the nature of the waves as well as the wind if you are going to sail in a desired direction. The dynamic movements of water and wind take every ounce of wisdom, courage, and skill to navigate.

Like the movement in the oceans and seas, your emotions and thoughts rise and fall, creating the crest and valley of each wave, tossing you about and challenging you to sail calmly through life's unexpected events. As a sailboat is built for water, so the human body is built for emotion. Emotions call for movement by their very nature. The root of the word itself, e-motion, *is* movement, and there are three basic ways that human beings move with emotions – suppress, express, and release. It is the beliefs we have about any emotion determine which of these three movements we will choose.

Suppressing Emotions

My experience with clients has taught me that most people hold some negative beliefs about the emotions of anger, sadness, and fear. In this model, thinking that there is something wrong with feeling an emotion, is similar to thinking there is something wrong with waves in the ocean. If we believe that an emotion is in some way bad, wrong, or not allowed, one way we may deal with it is to suppress it, holding it inside. In this sailboat model, holding in an emotion creates the dip or trough of a wave in your ocean of emotion. Any change to the ocean rocks our boat, and sailing calmly becomes more challenging.

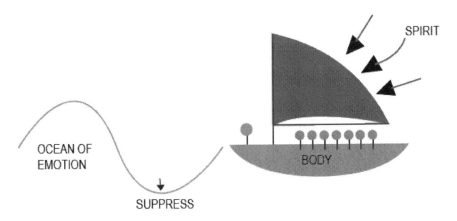

Holding an emotion, especially for long periods of time, is expensive to the physical body. When we hold onto an emotion from a past event, we pay with a bit of our vital life energy in order to contain it. As we suppress an emotion, it wears out some aspect of our physical body. According to the principles of Chinese medicine, emotional suppression directly affects specific organs in the body, depending upon the emotion. For example, suppressing an emotion like frustration or anger agitates the liver and gall bladder and may create headaches, joint pain, irregular heart rhythm, or fibrous tumors. Held sadness and grief impact the lungs, colon, and the skin, possibly manifesting as patterns of bronchitis, asthma, constipation, or psoriasis. The bottom line is that when an emotion is suppressed, its energy creates havoc somewhere in our body's health.

Rachel (not her real name) came to my office after many years of suppressed emotions started taking their toll on her health. She had grown up in a family that believed children should be quiet, compliant, and pleasant. Confrontation or displays of anger were an absolutely not allowed. Taught to hold any objections, Rachel was considered a good daughter. No one in her family either expressed or discussed their feelings. Now in her early 50's, Rachel had swallowed a lot of emotion from living with these beliefs and the suppression they demanded. Her body began showing the strain of this holding in with symptoms of high blood pressure, irregular heart rhythms, and chronic stomach pain. After her physician found no direct physical cause, he suggested that her symptoms were caused by stress and referred her to my office. Working together over time, Rachel became aware that shortly before the onset of any of these symptoms, an interaction with someone had left her feeling trapped and unable to confront the issue at hand. The "stress" her physician had pointed to was more accurately a pattern of emotional suppression. With this new awareness, we began working to shift her beliefs so that she could trust her emotions and allow herself to speak up on her own behalf in these interactions. Once she began to share her feelings, her blood pressure and heart rhythm returned to normal and the pain in her stomach disappeared. Rachel was amazed at how quickly and immediately her body changed once she stopped suppressing her emotions.

Expressing Emotions

If we believe that an emotion is good, right, or allowed, we may act it out or express it, drenching others in its energy. While expressing our emotions may sound like a positive choice, I use it here to describe a pattern that brings no lasting resolution. This option often creates a *temporary* feeling of relief but does little to address the issue or change the pattern. Emotions that are allowed to openly run wild create the opposite imbalance as those in which emotions are suppressed. While suppression of emotion pushes the water in our ocean of emotion downward, expression causes it to rise into the crest of the wave. The bigger the expression, the higher the wave, and the more our boat is tossed about.

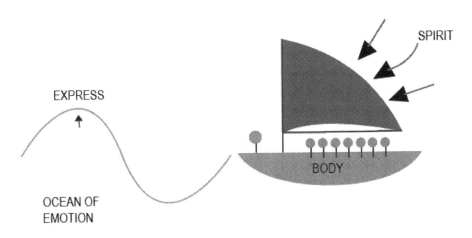

When our beliefs give us free rein to express emotions continually, it is often quite damaging to our relationships with those who endure or witness it. Like thunderstorms that roll through on a hot summer day, intense emotional displays may temporarily clear the air, but the lightning strikes do long term damage. This damage not only affects those around us, but repeated expression of emotion can do as much harm physically to our own body as suppression. Looking again through the window of Chinese medicine, living in a state of anxiety or chronic fear directly affects the kidneys and the bladder. This exhausts and potentially undermines the body so that low back pain, frequent urination, hearing loss, or fertility issues are among the symptoms that may arise. Battered about by the waves of emotional expression, our body boat takes a beating. Like suppression, expression does not create calm.

Riding the Waves of Suppressing and Expressing

By midlife, the call from within to change and grow signals a need to deal with our emotional patterns of the past. If our pattern has been one of repeated expression, we may find ourselves gradually feeling isolated or abandoned by people who have grown weary of our emotional displays. By midlife we may have lost friends, ended relationships, or been fired from jobs as others are no longer willing to deal with our outbursts. If we swing from expression to suppression, depression is frequently the outcome.

If our pattern has primarily been one of suppression, by midlife the effort needed to hold in the cumulative emotional energy becomes much greater. Over time, we may find holding emotions within has wreaked havoc in our physical or mental health. Like trying to hold a beach ball under water, suppressing emotion takes an enormous amount of attention and energy. As we continue to push them down, more of our energy is needed and consumed. At some point, our psychological arms get tired and rather than being able to allow the ball to surface in a gentle and controlled manner, it shoots out from under the water in a random direction, damaging ourselves or hitting an unintended target. Emotions suddenly erupt in unexpected or disproportionate ways. We know this when we overreact to a current situation. The emotion may be accurate for the event, but its intensity is driven by the energy of similar emotional experiences suppressed in the past. Our emotional wave has now swung from suppression to expression, again rocking our boat.

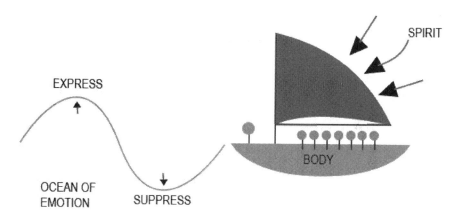

Swinging from suppression to expression is a very common pattern, and was clearly what my client Stewart (not his real name) had been doing most of his life. His father became an alcoholic before Stewart was born. Growing up with a brother and sister, Stewart learned quickly to prepare each night for the time when his dad came home from work. His father worked at a nearby steel mill doing a hard and dirty job that he hated. At the close of most workdays, his father and co-workers stopped at the neighborhood bar for a few drinks.

By the time he arrived home, he was drunk or close to it. Loud arguments with Stewart's mother were the 6:00 pm routine. As a child, Stewart hid in his bedroom closet, pushing his fingers into his ears to block the sound of his parents' fighting. Once he grew into a strong and strapping teen, he could no longer tolerate the daily alcohol-driven bickering and began physically fighting with his father. Moving into romantic relationships in his adult life, Stewart had a hard time being affectionate. When angry, he frequently would swallow his feelings, then later lash out after some small slight or injustice. He felt confused about what to do with any emotion he experienced. Stewart was 42 years old when he came to my office looking for a way to make peace within, hoping to end this vacillation between the emotional extremes of suppression and expression.

Releasing and Resolving Emotions

It is easy to see that neither suppression nor expression of our emotions produce lasting peace or calm within. What we are looking for is a way to release the waves of emotion, allowing them to resolve into smooth and placid waters. Emotions that we do not like, we frequently wish would just go away. People use any number of external methods to help sedate these feelings – cigarettes, alcohol, drugs, TV, electronic devices, work, shopping, food, sex, or excessive exercise. We think that if we could just stop the emotions, life would be so much easier. If only I could control my anger. If only I could end my anxiety. If only I could escape my sadness. The reality is that emotions are the water on which we sail the seas of our life. Emotions inform us of the changing dynamics of our experience. Avoiding an emotion denies us access to the information it is trying to convey. A far better approach is to recognize and understand that an emotion is a movement within us, ask what the emotion needs, and allow the energy it holds to move us in that direction.

If we think of emotions as neither good nor bad, neither right nor wrong, but simply as providing us with information about our experience, we give ourselves the chance to understand their message and make wise decisions on how to use their energy. This third option offers us the most powerful outcome. When we view an emotion as neutral information, we have the opportunity to experience it, reflect upon its implication, and calmly choose a course of action. With this option, we can release the energy it holds, creating a calm and clear experience of resolution for all involved.

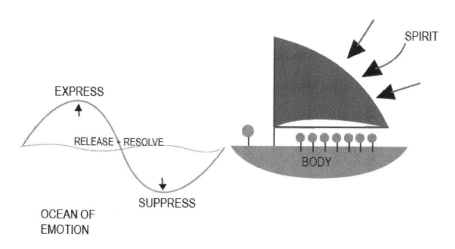

Releasing emotion in a state of calm through clear communication is a challenging skill, but one well worth mastering. It requires consciously *acknowledging* rather than denying the wave of emotion we are experiencing. It requires consciously *moving into*, rather than away from the feeling within. If we move toward the emotion with curiosity and without judgment, we create the opportunity to listen more deeply to the information the emotion offers. Creating calm requires that we neither suppress nor express the emotion, but rather seek to understand what each emotion is trying to tell us.

So what does an emotion attempt to tell us? And what does the emotion need? Let's look at the three that most of us avoid. The emotions of *anxiety or fear* tell us that we do not feel safe. We feel threatened by something or someone, real or imagined. Fear wants us to either remove the threat or seek safety. Feelings of *frustration or anger* inform us that something is not fair and want us to take action to create equity or a more balanced arrangement of reciprocity. *Sadness or grief* indicates that we have experienced a loss. Grief seeks reunion with what was lost or the acceptance that what was lost is no longer available to us. Each emotion sends a signal about our experience in a particular circumstance and asks for a resolution so that its energy can be released and resolved.

Releasing and resolving is best accomplished when we are settled into our body, our boat. Releasing and resolving are not possible if we allow ourselves to flail about in the waves of suppression and expression. Getting back in our boat is the key move that we will discuss later.

The Waves and Whirlpools of Thought

On the other side of the boat we find waves and whirlpools in the sea of thought. At the crest and trough of the waves, we ride the thoughts that are voiced in the absolutes of always and never. In this model, thoughts that contain *never* – "I must never be selfish" – push the sea downward, creating the trough of the wave. Thoughts that contain *always* – "I must always put others first" – push upward and create the crest of the wave. Oscillating thought waves now start to rock our boat.

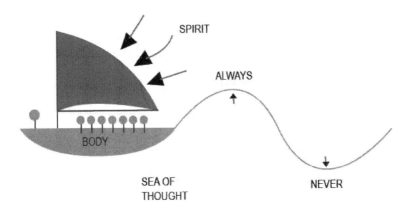

Steve (not his real name), age 46, was stuck in a pattern of negative reaction. To his wife Melissa, it seemed that whenever she had a new idea or made a suggestion, Steve's first response was always "no". If they were grocery shopping and Melissa suggested they purchase steak for dinner, Steve disagreed, saying he wanted fish. If they were driving to a friend's home and

Melissa wanted to take a particular route, Steve generally said he was going a different way. As often happened, 15 minutes later Steve would "come to his senses" as Melissa described, and agree to the original suggestion. After 10 years of marriage, Melissa was finding herself more and more frustrated with Steve's initial negative responses. At Melissa's urging, Steve came to see me for a session and we spent some time exploring his "always say no first" pattern.

The absolutes of always and never are usually established in childhood along with many of the other subconscious beliefs that run our system. Some of these are formed even before we develop language and are integrated into our mind/body matrix experientially. Years later, we may have an unconscious visceral reaction to a present situation that is really based upon an event that happened decades ago. In our work together, Steve quite vividly recalled the dynamics with his older sister Marsha. Born 11 months apart, Marsha was always stronger and more capable than Steve, so that even as toddlers, Marsha continually took whatever toy or object Steve found. Though he fiercely protested, their mother generally sided with his sister, and Steve was forced to give up what he wanted. Now in midlife, the pattern of saying no first had become his unconscious way of trying to get his own way. This old belief was replaying in present time and aggravating his relationship with his wife Melissa.

In his book *The Biology of Belief*, Dr. Bruce Lipton suggests that approximately 95% of our daily routine and behaviors are run by our subconscious mind. Our conscious mind, which resides in the part of our brain known as the prefrontal cortex, processes approximately 40 environmental impulses per second. By comparison, the subconscious mind that inhabits the rest of our brain processes some estimated 20,000,000 impulses in the same blink of an eye! Whatever we have stored in our subconscious is in essence *millions of times more powerful* than what we are consciously thinking. No wonder it is so difficult and takes such work to change the habitual behaviors we *know* are not good for us, but feel powerless to transform!

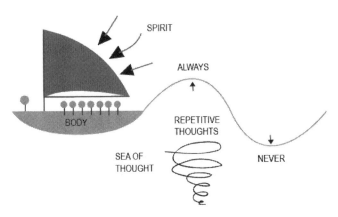

Thoughts also become more powerful as they get reinforced and repeated, replaying again and again in our head. When negative thoughts become repetitive, they become like whirlpools pulling us downward, dragging us to the depths of the sea. Around and around we go as the repetitive thought swirls continually within us. Perhaps the most common of these is "I am not good enough." This negative and undermining thought, often established very early in life, acts like a weight that drains us of our courage and confidence, then carries us to the bottom of the ocean, killing all manner of creativity. Freeing yourself from this whirlpool is well worth whatever efforts it takes.

As we saw with the ocean of emotion, the surging extremes of express and suppress must settle into a calmer wave. So too our sea of thought containing the absolutes of *always* and *never* must shift into a middle way. The thoughts of this middle way include words like maybe, perhaps, and sometimes. Always and never are rarely appropriate for every situation.

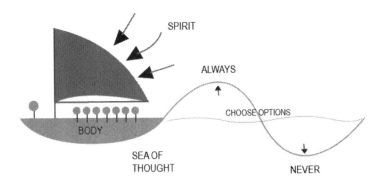

Having the option to *choose* our thought response based on what is *actually happening* in our life rather than being run by our subconscious beliefs from the past is necessary for living a satisfying life. To do this, we must wake up our attention, climb out of the waves of our incredibly capable but often dreadfully outdated beliefs in the absolutes, and use our conscious brain to think about what we want to create in this present moment.

It takes courage to go inward and usually takes us back to experiences in our childhood for the source of these outdated beliefs, but it does not take much time to find them. In midlife, we only have to look at any aspect of our life that we feel is not working well, and we will find an old and unproductive thought running the show. Our outdated beliefs are really the sunken treasure in our sea of life. Once raised to the surface from the depths of our subconscious, these beliefs revealed in the light of day become dazzling resources that can transform our journey ahead with their new freedom of choice we have never before had.

Get Back in Your Boat!

Waves on the ocean of emotion and sea of thought in midlife can toss our boat about so much that we can feel like we are *nothing but* emotion and thought. We find we cannot control or turn them off. Our thoughts and feelings consume us and we literally feel as though we are drowning in them. It is as if our body, our sailboat, does not even exist. Indeed, at that moment, our attention has jumped ship. We have allowed our attention to leap into the waves of emotion and thought, completely abandoning our boat.

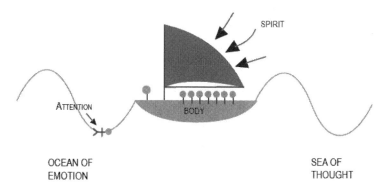

Floundering about in the ocean and sea, we have lost our sense of self. There is one and one thing only to do. GET BACK IN THE BOAT! COME BACK TO YOUR BODY! Captain Awareness needs to drag your attention out of the water and back to your body boat. The key is to do something – *anything* – that takes you into the physical experience of your body. Give your body your *full* attention. Notice what you feel in your body and where you feel it. Do something physical. The fastest and most readily accessible option is to breath deeply. Focus on relaxing and breathing into your belly, making your exhale twice as long as your inhale. Slowing your breath is simple, free, and an option that is always available. Do *whatever you can* do to get reconnected to your body. Stretch. Walk. Dance. Take a shower. Literally any movement that brings your awareness back into your body will do. Engaging your physical body *is the key* to getting out of the endless waves and whirlpools of thought and emotion.

In the 1960's, psychiatrist Fritz Perls created a counseling theory called Gestalt therapy. This approach invited the client to become aware of the physical manifestation of their emotions by asking the questions "What is happening right now? What am I experiencing?" The same idea is found in the Buddhist practice of being in the present moment. The present moment is *literally* what is happening right now. When I ask clients these questions, it invites them to look inward, giving them time to notice the sensations in their physical body. Becoming aware of their body rather than their emotions or thoughts, clients get out of the waves and back in their boat. This creates a pause in the internal turbulence. In this pause lies the opportunity of creating something different. It offers the chance to get out of old repetitive patterns of emotion and thought.

Once you have gotten back in touch with your body, take a few minutes to sit with these two questions: "What kind of body-centered self-care do I need *right now* to create calm? What is available *at this moment*?" Body-centered self-care adds ballast to your boat and brings you back into balance for a steadier sail.

Ballast for Your Boat

Ballast in a sailboat is a weight that is added at the bottom of the boat to keep it from tipping over. In strong waves or winds, it helps to stabilize and steady the boat so that it remains upright and afloat. There are numerous creative ways to add ballast, but the bottom line is that your sailboat needs it.

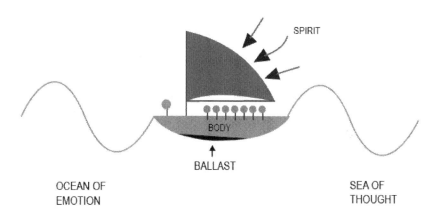

In our sailboat model, ballast represents any form of body-centered self-care. Over the years, I have looked for simple self-care tools that meet the following characteristics: quick, easy, effective, and free. In my opinion, the best of these focus on breath, rest, and movement, and can be done virtually anywhere. When not at home and some privacy is needed to stretch and shake out the tension of a thought or emotional pattern, you can find plenty of room in the handicap stall of public bathrooms. Here are my favorite things to add ballast to your boat and stabilize your life:

Breath – Your breath is the most powerful tool you own. Use it consciously to connect to your body and create a calm flow in and out. Start with a deep exhalation, contracting your abdomen to push the air all the way out. Relax your abdomen and draw air all the way down and into your belly, then fill your ribs and chest. Breathe slowly in and out, feeling the sensations throughout your torso. For the greatest impact, make your exhale twice as long as your inhale. Pausing at the end of each inhale and exhale also deepens the connection to your breath.

Movement – *Walk* – the rhythm of your steps while walking are grounding and settling. This is perfect ballast for your boat. *Dance* – moving to music can add an emotional connection and offer your body the chance to release even more. *Shake* – be creative and just shake every part of your body. Start with your feet and ankles and move on up. It may look or feel a bit strange, but this is a fabulous way to release patterns of holding created by emotion and thought. After a squabble, birds, dogs, and other animals will literally shake their whole body. They are releasing the energy of the fight. For thousands of years, shaking has been used as medicine in traditional cultures. *Exercise* – jogging, running, weight training, yoga, Tai chi, – all are perfect to shift out of emotion and thought. Also, there is nothing more satisfying than driving golf balls to transform anger, so check out your local driving range. Be creative, but move!

In his book *Unstuck,* psychiatrist Dr. Jim Gordon, of the Center for Mind-Body Medicine in Washington, DC, devotes an entire chapter to describing in great detail how he uses movement to help clients climb out of depression. In group therapy sessions, he puts on a CD of drum music and asks group members to shake out their physical tension and wake up their energy to the beat before beginning the counseling discussions. He also notes research that suggests exercise is more effective than Prozac in the long run.

EFT – Emotional Freedom Technique or EFT is a simple protocol for physically tapping on nine acupuncture points on the head and torso, while verbally addressing emotional and physical pain. Discovered by clinical psychologist Roger Callahan, refined by Gary Craig, and now marketed worldwide by Nick and Jessica Ortner, EFT tapping creates movement in the energy flow of the body, releasing patterns that lead to disease and pain. EFT is among a growing number of modalities in the new field of energy psychology. If you have not seen it in action, google EFT or any of the names above and follow the links to their sites. You will also find a number of different forms of tapping protocols using a variety of points. I suggest you start with the nine points used by the Ortners. You can learn how to tap these nine points in just a few minutes. The EFT protocol includes saying aloud the negative beliefs that you hold, and accepting yourself as you have them. The tapping continues with saying the positive beliefs you want to instead make part of your belief system. Even without the verbal aspect, tapping the points sends a calming signal to the fight-or-flight part of the brain called the amygdala. The results from use of EFT are at times miraculous.

Clean whole foods and plenty of water – There is no shortage of information about the importance of eating whole foods and drinking enough water. Food is our first medicine, but making dietary changes are some of the toughest changes to make. Hire a coach – a nutritionist, dietician, functional medicine practitioner - someone to help you make a plan and stick to it.

Sleep and rest – Get enough. Eight hours is still what is recommended for the majority of human beings. Find a way to go to bed a little earlier. Turn off the electronics an hour before bedtime. Light some candles and enjoy the ambience instead. Many in midlife find that they wake up somewhere around 3:00 am with ruminating thoughts of worry or indiscriminate feelings of anxiety. If this happens to you, the middle of the night is the ideal time to align your body with your spirit. Turn onto your back, rest your hands on your heart and abdomen, and shift your attention to your physical body. Starting at your head and neck, progressively relax each area of your body, allowing it to sink more deeply into the mattress. Now focus on your breath using the long, slow exhale I described above. Once your body has further settled with the breath, take your awareness to whatever spiritual practices you hold. Repeating a prayer or mantra, breathing out with the word *peace*, or imagining you are being held in the palm of a loving or divine being can easily set the stage for a return to sound sleep.

Legs-up-the-wall pose – A fabulous way to rest without sleeping is a resting pose from yoga called legs-up-the-wall. Get down on a carpeted floor, scoot your buttocks up against the wall, and swing your legs straight up the wall so that they are now vertical and perpendicular to the floor. Changing your relationship with gravity allows the arch in your low back to ease and the blood in your legs to flow effortlessly back to your heart. Lie there for 10 minutes, breath deeply and rest. This is one of the most amazing tools I have ever found, especially if you are on your feet a good portion of the day. I do this several times throughout the day whenever I am cooking a big meal for a holiday or standing for a long period of time. Legs-up-the-wall is also superb just before going to bed, setting the stage for deep, restful, and stress-free sleep.

Hot bath – Another way to rest is in the bathtub, the most underused stress relief tool in your home. Living in our hurry-up-and-shower culture means that we miss the benefits of completely relaxing in a pool of warm water. Fold a full-sized bath towel and put it in the bottom of the tub for extra cushion. Light a candle and add some Epsom salts if you'd like. Give yourself 15 minutes to soak, breathing deeply and consciously letting go of the tension in your body.

Apps – Lastly, in today's world of smart phones, there is an amazing array of apps that can help guide you through a breathing practice, meditation, or yoga sequence. Video resources for these same practices abound on the Internet and at the public library. The *best* self-care ballast for your boat is the one that *you will actually use*. So find what works for you and build it into your lifestyle.

From Intention to Action

Adding ballast to stabilize your boat requires moving from intention to action. In midlife, it is even more essential that we take action to create what we intend. When we say that we "intend" to change or that we will "try" to change some aspect of our habits, but do not have a clear plan, we often fall short of that which we say we want. Working with clients, I regularly ask "What is your intention for this session?" They choose a word or phrase that captures the essence of what they want to create. Peace. Calm. Serenity. Acceptance. Compassion. Letting go. Deep rest. If they want to create this more fully in their life, some action beyond the session is necessary. If they want peace, I ask for a very specific behavior that will help them to experience it. They might choose prayer or meditation, being out in nature, or a quiet breath practice. We determine the day of the week, time of the day, length and frequency of the practice that will best serve them. With specific details made clear, I then inquire how they would like to hold themselves accountable. This is where they often become a little uncomfortable, and resistance starts to emerge. Most of us do not like the idea of being held accountable, even for something that we really want.

During an integrative bodywork session, Denise (not her real name), a female client in her 40's, shared that taking a hot bath once a week would be a wonderful and easy way to reduce her stress physically, mentally, and emotionally. We discussed the best time of the day, day of the week, and ways to make the bath experience more restful. Since she was unsure if she would actually do this each week, I suggested a creative and optional agreement. The agreement stated Denise would take a 20-minute hot bath every week until her next appointment. For each week that she did not take the agreed upon bath, she would pay me $100. Denise laughed, saying it was a great idea to help her to keep her commitment to herself, and signed a written copy of the agreement. Eight weeks later she returned with the agreement listing the dates of her eight weekly baths. Delightfully, she was able to move beyond her resistance to self-care, holding herself accountable, and owing me nothing. This simple shift made it possible for her intention to become action.

Sometimes, removing the obstacles that get in the way is the shift needed. I discovered yoga in the 1990's and loved it immediately. Nothing made me feel as clear, grounded, calm, and strong. The change I felt from an hour's class was nothing short of miraculous, and I wanted to create a practice on my own at home. At first I kept my yoga mat in a closet, but soon found that out of sight meant yoga at home didn't happen. Having grown up as a Roman Catholic, I had been taught to "avoid the near occasion of sin." One afternoon that phrase came back into my recall and it occurred to me that if I changed a few words, I could use the concept to "invite the near occasion of yoga." As an experiment, I decided to leave my mat in the center of the living room floor as an invitation to more frequent yoga. Many days I walked past the mat on my way to do the laundry. My head ran through the list of all the things I had to do before I had time to do yoga. (Remember, "Work first. Rest later.") The inner battle between my head's list of chores and my body's desire to stretch ensued. At first, my head won. One afternoon I paused and put one foot on the mat. It seemed to pull the rest of me on like a magnet. Once there, actually doing yoga was easy. It seemed to me that the trick from turning this intention into a kept commitment meant I needed to remove all resistance to getting my feet on the mat.

I started removing resistance by storing a mat under my bed. Each morning when I woke up, I would reach under and slide out the mat. Then I would get out of bed. There it was and I was standing on it! All obstacles to getting on the mat were removed. Amazingly, doing a daily yoga practice became quite easy.

Now this may seem like an absurdly long and tedious process. Why, you may wonder, did she not just take NIKE's advice and "just do it"? I certainly have wondered the same. But having listened to thousands of other regular and ordinary people describe their own attempts to make self-care changes, I have come to appreciate that this process is very common. Shifting from intention to action can be very simple if we allow ourselves a bit of creativity. Shifting from having an intention to taking action also requires that we develop a strong commitment to loving and caring for ourselves. This is not something that most of us do naturally. It takes a bit of work and generally in the beginning, we benefit from some outside support. In our sailboat model, it means calling on the some aspect of the wind or breeze – meaning, purpose, connection, community, and creativity.

Using the Tools of the Boat and the Breeze

In early February, Sarah (not her real name), age 35, called for a session to see if she could change her disturbed sleep pattern and lift her feelings of depression. She had begun a PhD program the previous fall at a nearby university. She was eating well, got frequent exercise, and had regular contact with a few friends who were also going through the PhD program. Quiet and soft-spoken, Sarah described herself as a good listener. By the end of the fall semester, she had become depressed. Over the holiday season, her depression had increased and now she was not able to sleep through the night. She had seen her physician, but did not want to use medication, and had agreed to talk with a counselor. Hearing that food intake, movement, and social contact seemed appropriately in place, I asked what she had been noticing in her thoughts. Were there any thoughts that seemed negative or repetitive? Sarah described her mind as feeling anxious about what others thought of her. She believed that other people felt sorry for her and said they liked her when they really did not. With further discussion, Sarah admitted that *she* did not like *herself.* Even more fundamentally, she felt that her life did not really matter.

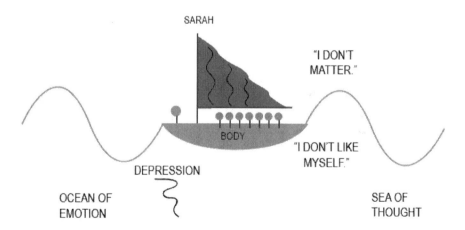

Sarah's Boat – Hearing this, I invited her to sit back in her chair, close her eyes, and drop her awareness into her body. I asked her to notice what she was feeling at that moment and where the sensation was located in her body. She described her shoulder feeling slumped and rounded and her chest sunken and heavy. She said her legs felt tightly contracted. I asked her to now pay attention to her breath, allowing the inhalation deep into her belly.

For a few minutes, I guided her through a simple relaxation breath exercise, while inviting her body to soften and shift more and more into a place of comfort with each exhalation. Within a few minutes, Sarah reported that she physically felt much better – more open, relaxed, and calm. This practice of dropping into the body and attending to the breath is the return to the boat.

Sarah's Breeze – Next, I invited her to stand and walk around the room, letting her body move freely, stretching to release any areas that still felt heavy, depressed, tense, or tight. (Note: I always join with the client in this movement so that they don't feel self-conscious or embarrassed.) With her body relaxed and open, I next invited Sarah to say out loud, "I don't matter." Immediately she noticed that her legs felt tight, and shoulders dropped forward, and her chest felt empty again. Continuing to walk, I suggested that she shake that feeling out of her body, again stretching, moving, and breathing until it released. Back in a neutral space, this time I invited her to say aloud, "I matter." Sarah immediately started to smile and giggle. She felt instantly lighter and more at ease just saying those two words. For a few more minutes she stretched and walked around the treatment room repeating, "I matter," smiling and giggling all the while. The delight in her face and ease in her body were unmistakable. Gone were the signs of depression. She remarked that she had never realized so clearly the connection between the thoughts and beliefs she held and what they created in her physical body.

Running a belief like "I don't matter" literally takes all the wind out of our sails. The spiritual dimension of our life gives us meaning and purpose. If we abandon meaning and purpose, we abandon ourselves. Embracing a belief like "I don't matter" does exactly that; we are giving up and literally throwing in the towel on ourselves, spiritually disconnecting from the essence of who we are. When we speak aloud a statement of value, connection, or purpose, we reestablish connection to our meaning and fill our sails once again with the breeze of spirit.

At the end of the session, I gave Sarah several practices to do at home to support this shift. First, on several post-it notes or index cards, I suggested that she write the statement "I matter", and tape one to the bathroom mirror and put the rest in places that she would see every day – wallet, computer, and kitchen windowsill. Whenever she saw the notes, I asked her to take just a moment to say the statement "I matter" aloud, breathe deeply, and smiling, shake out any tension in her body. Secondly, I encouraged her to write several times "I matter" in her journal every morning - first with her dominate hand, then with her non-dominate hand. The physical act of writing is another way to anchor the new belief into consciousness. Writing is a kinesthetic activity and physically creating the words make the belief more real. Also, writing with both hands engages both sides of the brain, helping both aspects to integrate this new belief.

I have worked with many other clients using the same process, sometimes simply having them assume the body posture of their undesired emotion. When they change their posture to one that is more open and relaxed, they can immediately feel the shift in their emotional state. In her research, social psychologist Amy Cuddy investigated the effect of using high power body positions like standing with your hands on your hips, and low power body positions like sitting slumped in a chair. She and her team found that putting your body in a high power position for *just two minutes* increased your body's level of testosterone, the assertiveness hormone, while decreasing your level of cortisol, the stress hormone. Likewise, holding a low power pose for two minutes increased cortisol while decreasing testosterone.

In another study by Cuddy, after holding the body positions for the two-minute period, participants then went into a job interview. Those who had used the high power positions were consistently evaluated as more capable, confident, and potentially a more desirable employee. Regardless of their background and training, those who used a low power position were rated lower in the same categories and were less often selected as the potential employee. I encourage you to watch her TED talk on the Internet as she presents her fascinating life story along with this research. It is quite inspiring!

You likely have had the experience of how changing your mind about an issue or concern changes the way you feel in your body. Even more amazingly, changing your body cannot only help to change your mind, but your body chemistry and the way you are perceived by others as well. When you consciously align your body and your mind in a positive way, you create the optimum conditions for the most positive outcome in whatever you are doing. Buddhist monk and world-renowned meditation teacher, Thich Nhat Hanh says it this way, "Sometimes I smile because I am happy. Sometimes I am happy because I smile." Or, said another way, "Sometimes my happiness is the cause of my smile. Sometimes my smile is the cause of my happiness."

Using the Boat and Breeze Model in Your Life

I have come to believe that one of the biggest tasks in adult life is getting in charge of where we put our attention. What are we paying attention to? Whatever has our attention also has our thoughts, directs our emotions, and consumes our energy. Mind and body intimately and absolutely flow together as one. (Think Mobius strip again.) The concept of mind goes beyond thought. It is what we are aware of and encompasses all that we are paying attention to. The duty of our very own Captain Awareness is to stay awake at the helm of our boat, carefully discerning how to attend to our physical and spiritual dynamics while skillfully navigating the waters of our emotion and thought.

Like an undisciplined child, our thoughts can run wild, exploring endless possibilities that include creating distress and exhaustion for the rest of our system. Like thoughts that are permitted to escalate, uncontrolled emotions can create the same kind of havoc, taking us out of the awareness that we even *have* a body. As human beings we have the capacity to focus. In our younger years, we may have been able to manage a wide range of distractions, allowing ourselves to be pushed and pulled in all different directions. In midlife, we no longer have that luxury as our life becomes more defined by increased responsibilities. Our time and energy become ever more precious. How we use our attention not only matters, but also determines the quality of our life and health. Consciously focusing our attention on what *really* matters to us, what we *really* want, becomes absolutely essential in midlife.

What we learn from the sailboat model is this – if we want to successfully sail the challenging seas and oceans of midlife, we *must* first wake up our awareness so that we can focus our attention. We *must* become aware of what we truly wish to create in our life. The moment we realize that we are floundering in the ocean of emotion or sinking in the sea of thought, we *must* take our attention back to our physical body and spiritual practices. We *must* get back in the boat of our body and bring the breeze of our spirit back into our sail. It is this *vertical* alignment of the boat and the breeze – *our body with our spirit* - that balances the wild ride created by our thoughts and emotions. It is this *body and spirit partnership* that allows us to sail smoothly and calmly onward.

Here are a few questions to help you reflect upon how you are sailing your own sailboat in the seas of your life. After answering these for yourself, you might consider asking a trusted friend to answer the same ones about you. It takes a great deal of courage to invite this kind of feedback, but it can be incredibly valuable. These questions are also excellent to discuss with your counselor or therapist.

1. How does your body communicate with you? Which crewmembers do you hear from the most? What do these areas say or need?

2. What is the *easiest and fastest* thing for you to do to get back in your body when you realize that you are lost in thought or sinking in emotion?

3. What is the most important ballast to balance your boat?

4. What inspires you and gives your life meaning, purpose, or value?

5. How often do you engage in activities that support your spirit?

6. How are you connected to others – groups, clubs, organizations, or communities?

7. What emotions are you most comfortable experiencing?

8. What emotions are you least comfortable experiencing? Do you suppress or express them?

9. Of your least comfortable emotions, would you be willing to explore releasing and resolving them in at least one situation?

10. Do you have enough support in processing emotions? Do you journal your feelings? Talk with a close friend? Work with a counselor?

11. Consider creating a short phrase to help you remember to return to your body and spirit like "Get back in the boat" or "Call in the breeze." What works for you?

The Drama Triangle

*"Our ultimate freedom is the right and power to decide
how anybody or anything outside of ourselves will affect us."*

- Stephen Covey

Growing up, I routinely watched a cartoon called "Dudley Do-Right of the Mounties." In it, a fiendish Snidely Whiplash had a favorite pastime of tying helpless folks, especially fair maidens, to railroad tracks. The dim witted but ever cheerful Canadian Mountie Dudley Do-Right and his horse would come to their rescue. Whiplash would eventually tie Nell Fenwick, daughter of Dudley's boss, to the tracks. Dudley, with his chest puffed and voice deepened, would confidently declare, "I'll save you Nell!" and off he would ride. The dynamics between these three characters remained predictable in every cartoon. Snidely would capture Nell. Dudley would save her and other damsels in distress. Snidely, grumbling, scurried off with "Curses! Foiled again!" to plan his next devious deed. We find this trio of characters – the bad guy, the rescuer, and the one being saved - in every good plot. Any movie called a drama will include players or elements that present these three qualities.

In 1964, Psychiatrist Dr. Eric Berne, creator of the psychological theory known as Transactional Analysis, published the book *Games People Play*. A worldwide bestseller, *Games* uncovered some of the fundamental dynamics in human relationships. Though the book was published over 50 years ago, the patterns of human behavior it reveals remain unknown to many. Like the proverbial elephant in the room, these patterns happen every day, right before our eyes, exhausting and confounding us in the dynamics of relationships. I was introduced to Transactional Analysis in my counseling theory courses, but it was not until I was in therapy myself a decade later that I came to understand the value this simple model offered as a tool for transforming my life.

A core part of Dr. Berne's psychological theory is called the Drama Triangle. In his triangle, the vertex points are labeled with the three players in human drama – villain, victim, and hero. (Think Whiplash, Nell, and Dudley.)

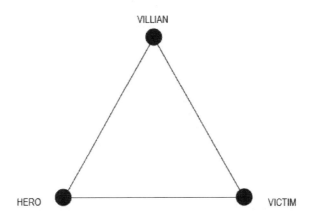

By the time we reach midlife, we have had plenty of experience with human relationships and, though we may not name them, we know these roles very well. It seems the triangle dynamics are simply a part of the human psyche, and you will find them anywhere and everywhere. While listening to people share their stories, you can identify the roles they play and often the ones they project on others. These roles are so common that I have come to consider the game of the drama triangle as *the game* that *everyone* on this earth is both playing and invited to transcend. Every time I listen to a client describe the difficulties they have in a relationship, then share this simple model, they throw up their hands saying, "That's exactly it! That is exactly what is happening!" Then they ask, "How do I get out of this?" First, we must look at each role and how we participate.

The Villain

The villain is likely the easiest to understand and the one we least want to be. The villain is the persecutor or bad guy who does wrong. He/she can show up as perfectionist, bulldog, competitor, or know-it-all. Excessively vigilant, he/she often keeps score in relationships. The villain runs over or pushes around others to get their own way. Emotionally, the villain may display righteous indignation, while pointing fingers of blame at others.

The Victim

The victim is also easy to spot. Presenting at times as a martyr, complainer, or rebel, the victim is the one who has been wronged. He/she may question or doubt all decisions. Or, to avoid making decisions all together, he/she may act like a space cadet. Victims often cling to their story of hurt and pain, retelling the sad story again and again. The emotions of shame, humiliation, and embarrassment also fortify this role.

The Hero

Though the hero sounds like a positive role, it is no better a position on the triangle than either of the other two. Its personas include the super competent, the caretaker, and the cheerleader. Heroes are the dependable ones. He/she rescues people and circumstances. The hero may be a martyr, but unlike the martyr/victim, he/she would complain less and likely have more personal energy. The negative aspect of this role is that the hero is trapped in the role of the do-gooder even when he/she would prefer not to assist.

The Triangle Dynamics

Once we understand the three roles, we find them all around us as we watch others interact. Listen to the conversations in the work lunchroom, in grocery lines, or better yet, at a cocktail party when inhibitions are loosened by alcohol. The relationship dynamics around the triangle follow this predictable pattern. A victim feels wronged by a villain. There is considerable tension or negativity between the two. To relieve the unwanted emotional feelings, the victim looks for someone or something to rescue them. Once found, the hero takes up the cause to defend or protect the victim by taking on the villain. Now the tension shifts from the villain/victim side of the triangle to the villain/hero side. The victim gets temporary relief.

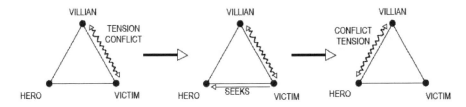

An example that is easy to understand is the dynamic between parents and child. Ten-year old Annie asks her mother if she can go to the movies with her friends. Her mother says no since Annie has not finished cleaning her room. Annie feels angry and unsatisfied, and goes to ask her father, who is unaware of the room cleaning responsibility and who does not consult with his wife. He says yes. Carefully avoiding her mother, Annie happily heads off to the movies with her friends. Now the tension and anger shift to between mom and dad. The disturbance in the triangle has shifted from the right side to the left side. This is one of the most common drama dynamics I hear in the stories my clients share.

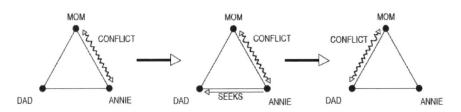

The triangle's drama can be more subtle as in the case of Sarah, Richard, and Mildred. After her husband died, Aunt Mildred moved in with Sarah and her husband Richard. Aunt Mildred loves to talk and loves having attention. Around the evening dinner table, Aunt Mildred frequently chatters on for an hour after the meal is finished. Richard has many things he needs to tend around the house and yard, but never wants to interrupt his aunt. He grew up with the belief that elders are to be respected, and that in all cases, their wishes come before his own. If Aunt Mildred wants to talk, he must listen without complaint. Richard frequently complains to Sarah about all the time he loses listening to Aunt Mildred's tales. After hearing his repeated complaints, one afternoon Sarah shares with her aunt that she needs not to talk so much at dinner, that Richard has work to do. Aunt Mildred feels insulted and controlled, and while she does begin to keep long conversations for another time, she becomes quite angry with Sarah. In the triangle dynamics, Sarah rescued Richard from Aunt Mildred. Richard was happily freed to move onto his projects, without needing to say a word. Now the tension is between Sarah and Aunt Mildred.

Another way the drama triangle can play out is when the villain is not a person, but rather a situation or a health condition. None of us want to find out that we have a disease or illness of any kind, but the nature of being human means that many of us will. What is our response? Do we collapse and allow the diagnosis and symptoms to run our life? Do we become a victim to the villain of disease? Do we expect the doctors and medical community to save us? Or do we hold our ground as a whole person, doing what we must to deal with the disease, making the necessary changes, while being as responsible and positive as we can be to live our life fully?

Those who develop a chronic disease and decide to join a support group must be especially mindful of the slippery slope into victimhood. Support groups built around a specific disease pattern can offer the chance to learn from others, both how they deal with symptoms as well as treatment options. At the same time, once a person makes the illness part of their identity, at some level, it may become necessary to maintain the disease to remain part of the group. This can be an especially difficult dynamic for those who were lonely before the disease. Because of the disease pattern, the support group in essence has rescued the person from the villain of loneliness. I was concerned about this dynamic when I heard one client with fibromyalgia refer to herself and others in the support group as "we fibros." What if she does heal? Would she have to give up the monthly meetings and the relationships in the group? Why get better if you will be out of the club and isolated again? Don't get me wrong. Support groups are wonderful, and are filled with people who understand what we are going through when others may not. Every day support groups help those struggling with issues of alcohol, drug addiction, trauma, and disease. We do though need to be actively aware of what we individually gain from any group and why we continue to participate. There can be a fine line between getting true support and forming an identity around being a victim.

We can use any number of things to rescue ourselves from something we don't like or want to avoid. Shopping, TV, alcohol, drugs, tobacco, excessive exercise, sleep, and the all-time favorite, food, are common choices to push away feelings we don't want to feel. Maybe we hate our job, and rather than do the hard work of exploring other options, we soothe ourselves each night with hours of TV and a big bowls of ice cream. Perhaps we are angry about being left out of a family event and don't know how to address it, so we go shopping for clothes we don't need or want in order to make ourselves feel better. One of my favorite ways to rescue myself was with dark chocolate. Feeling tired, overworked, or unappreciated, I would find myself standing in front of the pantry shelf reaching for a chocolate cookie. The villain of life had worn me out and I was having a little pity party for myself. Rather than lie down and rest for a while or just go to bed early, I would sedate my feelings with chocolate.

The Game Inside and Out

This game that Eric Berne so insightfully identified is played out not only in our relationships and in our choices, but also in our heads. We don't even need another human being or a variety of distractions to play. Our internal dialogues work much like the external ones. Just listen to your thinking. Let's say that you are packing for a trip to the beach for the annual family reunion. You start to recall the stressful dynamics between Uncle Leo and nephew Charlie at last year's gathering. Internally, the drama dialogue begins. Last year, you ended up with a headache. You felt they ruined the reunion experience for you and others. No one in the rest of family has been willing to talk with Leo and Charlie (villains) about their behaviors and you (victim) are feeling trapped with the anticipation of yet another week of having to listen to them bicker. Perhaps you will once again suffer in silence. You start to scheme about how you (hero) might control or arrange activities, meals, etc. in order to keep them apart to save everyone's vacation time from their negativity. The drama has begun in your head, and you are in the game before you even walk out the door.

Staying in the game of the drama triangle is ultimately isolating, disempowering, and exhausting. After presenting the drama triangle to a group at a retreat, one woman raised her hand and said simply, "I now realize that I spent all day Friday on the triangle going from one role to another." She got it. What a powerful realization!

Ending the Game

Once you understand the triangle, how do you stop the drama? If you want out of the drama triangle, there are two key questions to ask yourself: *What do you really want? Are you willing to do what it takes to make that happen?* Knowing what you really want takes work. Many folks spend their energy complaining endlessly about what they don't like or want. Ask them what they do want, and strange as it may seem, they are often clueless. Sorting out the options in a given situation and deciding what to pursue takes time and energy. Actually doing what it takes to make that choice happen requires work. Remaining in any of the roles – victim, hero, or villain – is often easier as it is both well established and familiar. Doing something different means change. To end the game, each player is invited to change by assuming responsibility for his or her own life experience. Gay Hendricks, in his book *Conscious Living*, states that each of us must assume *100% responsibility* for the outcome of our choices. This is a clear and tall order in midlife.

For those who do want to free themselves, each role has a way to slide off the triangle and get out of the game. In his Transactional Analysis model, Eric Berne also named the choices and behaviors that end the game and set us free. Let's see what Berne says each player needs to do to create autonomy.

From Hero to Supporter

For the hero to end the exhausting job of rescuing, he/she must slide out of the role into the healthier one of *supporter*. We all need assistance at times. None of us gets through life on our own. But there is a significant difference between supporting and rescuing. If we pay attention to our body, we can usually feel the difference physically. When we offer support without overdoing it, we feel energized or even refreshed by the opportunity to serve another. When we rescue and are doing more than is appropriate for the other person, we initially may feel our ego get a boost, but over time we may feel exhausted by it. Whether we volunteer or are asked again and again to assist, we may feel increased resistance or a sinking feeling of dread as the signal that we are becoming trapped in the rescuer role occurs. This is the time to pause and re-evaluate our beliefs about our choices. Paying attention to how we feel in our body can inform us if we have crossed the line from being a supporter to being a hero. In shifting off the drama triangle to the supporter, we must learn to listen to that place in ourselves that says "I have done enough," stopping there and doing no more. As a hero becomes a healthy supporter, they learn to *limit* how much they give away to others so that they have something left for themselves. Setting a limit on support also says to those playing the victim role that we have confidence in their ability to handle, deal with, or adapt to the issue at hand.

A subtle but simple example of this came into my awareness some years ago when I received a phone call from a friend asking me to give my time to a project that they were spearheading. At that time I was still making my way out of the "others come first" belief and had an immediate sense of hesitation, as well as a feeling of obligation to say "yes" on the spot. Fortunately, I had begun to work with my own midlife shifts and was able to take a deep breath, saying that I would give it some thought and get back to them the next day. As the phone call ended, I felt a huge sense of relief that I had given myself time to sort out how I really wanted to respond. Factoring my own needs into the equation of my response made all the difference in the world. After further reflection, I was able to find a time in my schedule and a contribution to the project that worked for me as well as my friend.

The physical feeling of hesitation informs us either that saying an immediate "yes" is *not* in our best interest, or that the specifics of the request may not be *completely* agreeable to us. The feeling of hesitation often manifests as a sinking or contraction in the chest and abdomen. Sometimes there is even a full body experience of tingling or heat running through our nervous system. Paying attention to our body's response can inform us as we approach the line where we are at risk of sliding back onto the triangle as a hero. This behavior of doing too much for others, of feeling obliged to assist, or of not knowing how to say no, is *the most common difficulty* I have seen, especially for women in midlife. Pausing, asking yourself "What do I really want?" and then setting a limit on how much you agree to is *the key move* to maintain the role of supporter.

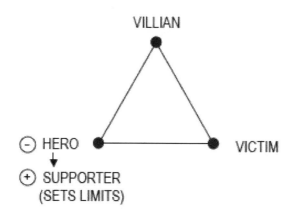

Brenda is another good example of a hero who was able to shift into the role of supporter. Raising four children, Brenda had always done the entire family's laundry as part of her role of wife and mother. She washed mountains of clothing every week and recently realized she had created a situation that needed to change. Brenda's oldest daughter Nicole had recently graduated from high school and was about to begin courses at the local community college. Brenda knew it was time for Nicole to do her own laundry- another responsibility of adult life. She was aware that continuing to do Nicole's laundry was also doing too much for her. At first Nicole complained and her dirty clothes piled up, but Brenda remained firm. After a few weeks, Nicole stepped up to the plate, and began doing her laundry. Though tempted to give in, Brenda kept her boundary. Setting this new limit with her daughter gave Brenda a sense of relief and more time for other things around the house.

From Victim to Adapter

For the victim to end the disempowering job of collapsing, they must slide out of their role into the healthier one of *adapter*. Adapting means accepting that things are as they are. It means putting an end to the complaints about their circumstances. When we step into the drama triangle as the victim, we give away our power and allow ourselves to become needy. Others, especially those prone to playing the hero, can feel this pull. There is nothing wrong with having a need, and asking others for help. But this is quite different than

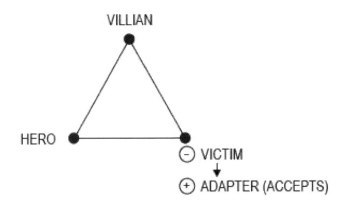

being needy. Instead of seeking the solution from others, the victim must decide what they are capable of doing to address the difficulty, stepping up to the plate to do what can be done. Sometimes this means letting their own efforts to address a need or situation be enough.

When you enter into the drama game as a victim, if you are paying attention, you can feel the change in your body. Can you hear the subtle whine in your tone of voice? Does your physical body slump or shoulders droop a bit when you talk about a certain issue? Are you secretly hoping that those listening to your story will take care of your concern for you? If so, you are agreeing to be a victim, and at the same time, looking for a hero.

One of the easiest ways that we can move out of the victim role is by changing the way we tell our story. When we simply stop talking about how we have been wronged, we stop fueling our victimhood. It does not mean that we remain silent about an issue that truly needs to be addressed. Rather, we change the way we speak about the difficulty. Instead of sharing all our pain and problems, we might speak about our strengths and the positive choices we are making in order to cope with the difficulty. This is a way of adapting to life as it is.

By midlife, it is likely that we have jumped in and out of the victim role many times. We have also observed others doing the same. The invitation of midlife is to assume full responsibility for the dealings of our life, adapting when necessary to the changes that come our way. When we slide off the role of victim with acceptance, we gain a sense of strength and peace that is never available as victim.

From Villain to Detacher

For the villain to end the isolating job of attacking, they must slide off the triangle into the healthier role of *detacher*. Detaching does not mean giving up or not caring. Detaching requires letting go of always having it our way, being large and in charge, or being the boss when it is not actually our job. Detaching means respecting others' opinions, contributions, and boundaries, finding common ground, and working toward a mutual agreement. None of us have all the answers all the time. When we believe or perhaps even insist that our point of view is the one that everyone else should adopt, we start stepping into the role of villain. If we are part of a team or group making decisions, detaching means allowing the ideas of the other members' time to be equally considered. Those prone to participating in the drama triangle as the villain often take on or are in leadership roles. Every good leader will at times need to make decisions that are viewed as unfavorable, but that does not make them a villain. Tough decisions sometimes need to be made and we know we cannot please everyone every time. Being a leader who is able to function in a healthy detached manner means giving it your all, but letting go of the outcome.

Those who are strong leaders in their workplace may find that bringing these same attitudes and behaviors home to family dynamics quickly puts them in the role of villain. One's role in the workplace is not the same role in the family. Family life does not run by the same organizational diagrams as the workplace. The degree to which we are considered "large and in charge" by those around us can give us a measure of how effective we are at jumping into or staying out of the role of villain.

In the role of the villain, we often feel strong and powerful. Our tone of voice may become louder and we might stand a bit straighter and taller. If we are paying attention to our body, we may notice that in this role we hold a level tension or contraction in the muscle along the back of our neck and spine. Though these physical changes may be subtle and hardly visible, they can be felt.

One way to use your body to detach from the role of villain is to take a deep breath and physically relax, dropping your shoulders and allowing your whole body to soften. Check you face, especially your eyebrows. Defending a villain position can move into an attitude of contempt, creating tension in facial expressions and causing us to raise one eyebrow. Research done by psychologist Paul Ekman, world expert on facial expression, reveals that the emotion of contempt is asymmetric and includes the raising of just one eyebrow. Most of us know this look as giving or getting the "evil eye." If you find you have stepped into the villain role, softening your face expressions and relaxing your body can help you to detach, moving into a more effective dynamic in your interactions.

When we detach from the villain role and slide off the triangle, we assume responsibility to see both sides of an issue even if we do not agree with the other side. We make room for understanding and compassion and the acceptance of paradox. This can soften us, help us to flow with circumstances as they arise, and bring pleasure back into our life. Letting go of the villain role, we speak our truth, but do not wage a battle either within ourselves or with anyone or anything in the outside world. Perhaps we take ourselves, and life, just a bit less serious.

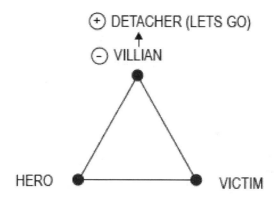

Villain, victim, and hero - these are the primary roles we play in the game of drama with others. In order to create more satisfying and healthy experiences in our relationships, we must slide off the triangle and out of the game as often as we find ourselves there. Deciding what we really want to create in a relationship, personal or professional, is the essential step. In *Conscious Living*, Gay Hendricks says we must take 100% responsibility for what shows up in our life. By midlife, we have had many years of experience exploring these roles and are in the perfect place to assume this level of responsibility, transforming our relationships as we end the drama game.

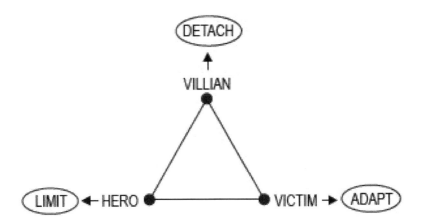

Putting it All Together ~ Creating Calm on the Rough Seas of Midlife

"I am not afraid of storms, for I am learning how to sail my ship."

Louisa May Alcott

Combining the three models together gives us a dynamic visual image for navigating midlife. Start with the model of the boat and the breeze. See the boat - your body - sailing on the ocean of your emotions and the sea of your thoughts. Your sail is a triangle, the Drama triangle. In order to adjust the sail to effectively catch the wind of your spirit and inspiration, you must loosen the ropes - your beliefs - which hold them in a given position. These ropes are tied down to the boat by weaving them around a metal cleat in a figure 8 pattern. Though not exactly the same, it looks very much like a Mobius strip. The beliefs you hold about being good or being enough are especially binding, tying down choices and limiting your options. Loosening these binding beliefs allows you to angle your sail effectively so that you can work with the winds of your spirit and the waters of your emotions and thoughts as they change.

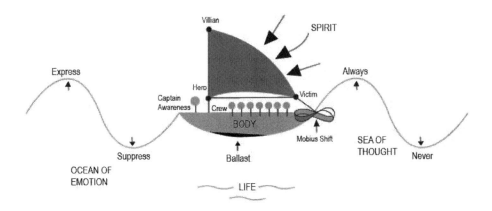

So there you are…sailing your body boat with the wind of spirit in your sails, riding the waves of the ocean of emotion and sea of thought. Your Captain Awareness and crew skillfully decide which belief lines of relationship dynamics to loosen to allow you to sail to catch the breeze so that you can move through midlife with ease and grace, in calm.

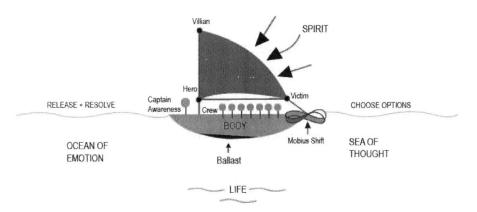

When you find yourself feeling challenged by some dimension of life, call up this dynamic image. Spend a few moments figuring out what needs attention. Think through these questions:

- Have you jumped ship and are you completely out in the water, floundering in the waves of emotion or thought? Do you need to get back in your body boat?

- What aspect of your body boat needs attention?
- Do you need more spiritual wind in your sails?
- Is there a tight belief line that needs to be loosened and adjusted?

As with sailing a boat, the dynamics of life are constantly in flux. Using this visual image as an overlay on your own life can help you to navigate calmly when you find yourself out in the open waters and rough seas of midlife. I encourage clients to put copies of this model where they will see it everyday as a reminder of the bigger picture needed to create calm. The bathroom mirror is a great spot since we all generally find ourselves in front of it, both at the beginning and end of the day. Put it in your appointment book, tape next to your computer screen, or lay it on the passenger seat of your car. These are all places that my clients have strategically placed copies to keep them mindful as they practice making these changes in their own life. You will find a larger version of the combined models in the appendix. I encourage you to make a few copies and spread them around in the places you frequent each day until these become so well known by your conscious mind that they drop into your subconscious mind, becoming part of your midlife navigational system.

The models and practices offered in this book have been gathered from my personal and professional experiences as an educator, massage therapist, counselor, and actually being the client of many therapies. In my work with students and clients, I have sought to support exploration, change, and growth with body-centered techniques and strategies that seemed appropriate, efficient, effective, simple, and inexpensive. I believe that good health requires tending to all of one's mental, emotional, physical, and spiritual needs. I also have come to believe that our ability to create a state of calm is essential for maintaining good health. Good health can be relatively inexpensive and quite simple. At the same time, it often seems difficult for most of us to choose and to sustain changes that support it.

The body's need for adequate sleep, movement, water, nurturance, and pleasure are often disregarded while beliefs about being accepted and valued by others speak louder than our sense of what we need. How did we come to disregard our very basic impulses that create a satisfying, and even joyful, healthy human experience? Thousands of books have already been written answering that question. One has only to explore the "self help" section of any bookstore to get a glimpse. Somewhere at the core of each of these literary works are two essential questions - "What do I really want? What do I believe about getting that?" All roads lead here. What do I believe about myself? My worth? My life? My goodness? On the long journey home to ourselves, our beliefs drive everything. And it is our beliefs about love, especially self-love, that matter most.

As I sit with those clients who are trying to navigate the waters of midlife, I have increasingly shared these three models. I present them as tools for the journey. I have also found these three models and practices to be the most valuable in my own exploration of the beliefs that were unconsciously driving choices and behaviors in my life. They have created the greatest understanding and most rapid shifts in my own patterns. Each model became a compass to help me release a belief that kept me from choosing something that was needed for better health in that moment. Each has helped me discover a belief submerged in the seas of my unconscious.

These models and practices lifted the veil that hid the beliefs within – the beliefs we operate on, but do everything in our power to avoid knowing. If we recognize the beliefs we operate from, we are immediately drawn into an incredible internal conflict. Make a change or suffer more. It is my belief that we are called to an ever more conscious way of living. As we become more conscious and change, we create less suffering. We create more ease and flow, more satisfaction and health. Raising the submerged beliefs of the past, which tie us up and hold us down, can be both scary and imperative for a healthy life.

Throughout this book I explored some of the concepts that I have discovered along the journey of self-care through midlife. It is certainly not all there is to consider or use, but it has included the concepts and practices that I have found highly effective for myself, my clients and students. I offer these three models as windows through which to view the dynamics in your own life. Clients and students have found these new perspectives to be a passage to moving beyond the sometimes depressive weight that comes with mature responsibilities of midlife.

At the end of the each integrative session, I ask clients how they feel. Their response is consistently " relaxed...lighter...more open...more calm." My clients have taught me that this is what I help them to create in their body and in their life. My hope is that these three models may in some way help you to create calm within, making your journey through the rough seas of midlife and beyond a smoother sail!

The Essential Keys

Have the courage

to go deep within

Your Body

and find

exquisitely laced within

every cell

Your Sacred Truths –

the essential keys

that will open

Your Life's Path

To

Freedom & Joy

Peace & Possibility.

- Vickii Engel Thomas, 2000

Appendix

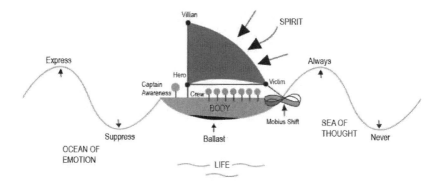

Get back in your body boat.

Call in the breeze of your spirit.

Shift your outdated beliefs.

End the drama by taking action to create what you really want.

Create calm on the sea of your life!

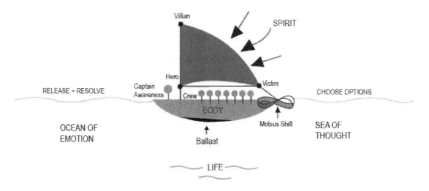

Bibliography

Ekman, Paul. *Emotions Revealed: Recognizing Faces and Feelings to Improve Communication and Emotional Life.* New York: St. Martin's Griffin, 2003.

Gordon, James. *Unstuck: Your Guide to the Seven-Stage Journey out of Depression.* New York: Penguin Books, 2008.

Hendricks, Gay. *Conscious Living: Finding Joy in the Real World.* New York: HarperCollins, 2000.

Lipton, Bruce. *The Biology of Belief.* Santa Rosa, CA: Mountain of Love/Elite Books, 2005.

Ortner, Nick. *The Tapping Solution: A Revolutionary System for Stress-Free Living.* Carlsbad, California: Hay House, Inc., 2013.

Rama, Swami. Ballentine, Rudolph., and Hymes, Alan. *Science of Breath: A Practical Guide.* Honesdale, Pennsylvania: Himalayan Institute Press, 1979.

Sheehy, Gail. *Passages: Predictable Crises of Adult Life.* New York: E. P. Dutton & Co. Inc., 1974.

Whitfield, Charles. *Boundaries and Relationships: Knowing, Protecting, and Enjoying the Self.* Deerfield Beach, Florida: Health Communication Inc., 1993.

Presentations and Appointments

Want to work with me? Would you like me to offer a presentation to your group, team, or staff? In addition to the topics offered in this book, I also present these on the following topics:

- Body Language – Understanding and Using Positive Nonverbal Communication
- Saying the Tough Stuff – How Your Body Can Help You Deliver Challenging Communications
- The Body as Portal for Conscious Change
- Breathing Well, Living Well
- Mindfulness Meditation and Living a Mindful Life
- Making Friends with Change
- Midlife – Shifting from Crisis to Transformation
- Self-care for Caregivers
- The Chakra Energy System as a Path to Create & Liberate

For group presentations, workshops, retreats, or individual sessions, you may contact Vickii at the following:

Vickii Engel Thomas, MS, LMT
The Center for Healing Arts
112 East Main St.
Westminster, MD 21157
410-848-9257 (office)
vickii@centerfor-healingarts.com
www.centerfor-healingarts.com

Made in the USA
Middletown, DE
04 October 2016